THE WAR
IN PICTURES

ODHAMS PRESS LIMITED
LONG ACRE, LONDON, W. C. 2

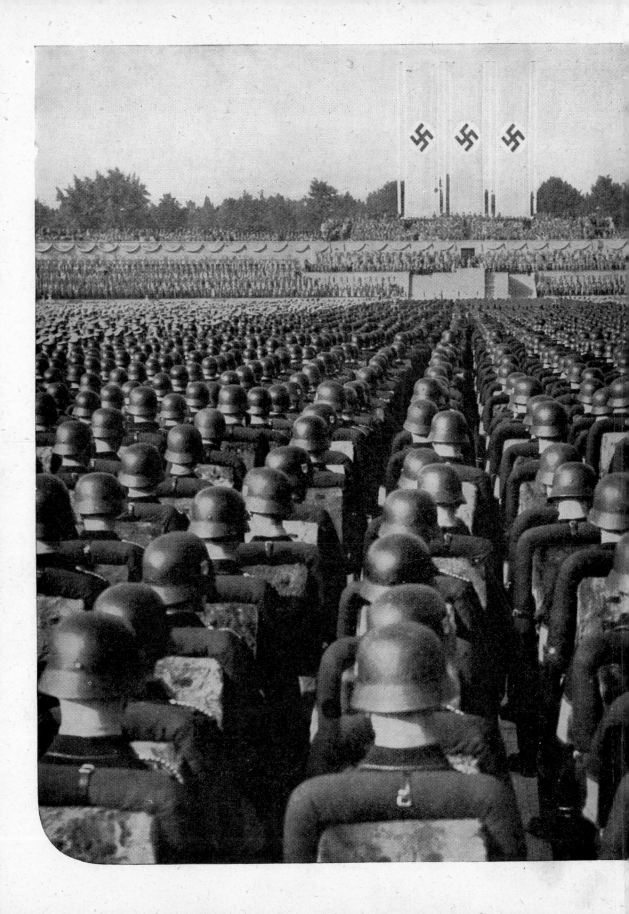

HOW THE WAR BEGAN

ON 3 September, 1939, the war clouds which had been temporarily dispersed at Munich a year before, burst, and Britain and France found themselves at war with Germany for the second time within a quarter of a century.

What were the reasons for this new clash of arms? Were they economic or imperialistic? Or was it because, as Hitler himself has said, the democracies of the west were decadent and that the first places in Europe must be taken by younger and more virile nations? The reader must form his own conclusions from the history of events that took place in Europe and elsewhere between the years 1918 and 1939.

At the end of the war of 1914-18 Germany, defeated in the field after four years and three months of the most bloody warfare the world had ever seen, was completely at the mercy of the victors. At Versailles, the statesmen of Britain and France were in no mood to deal leniently with their conquered foe. France, more than Britain, was determined to revenge the terrible suffering that had been inflicted on her people and her territory by the German invasion. Even so, the terms laid down were much less severe than those dictated by Germany to the Russians at Brest-Litovsk on 3 March, 1918.

In the Hall of Mirrors at Versailles, on 28 June, 1919, the German delegates listened in silence to the terms that were to be imposed upon their defeated country. Germany was to be stripped of large tracts of her most valuable industrial land; France, Belgium, Poland, Lithuania, Denmark and Czechoslovakia were all to share in the spoils. All her colonies were to be shared out amongst the Allies under mandates; the Rhineland was to be occupied by the Allies for fifteen years, and the Saar territory, a rich industrial and coal-producing district, was to be internalized. Germany was to recognize her sole war guilt and to pay reparations amounting to £6,000,000,000. In addition, complete disarmament, abolition of military service and military aircraft and the total

How the war began

destruction of armament factory equipment were demanded. The talons of the German eagle were to be effectively drawn.

There was, however, one aspect of this treaty that might have redeemed it—the birth of the League of Nations. The League was established under a covenant of twenty-six articles which formed Part I of the Treaty of Versailles. The Covenant bound member nations mutually to respect their independence and territorial integrity and not to employ force for the settlement of disputes until they had first submitted them to the League. Sanctions (i.e., military or economic measures intended to enforce the fulfilment of international treaty obligations) were to be taken against any country committing an act of aggression in defiance of the Covenant. According to Versailles, however, any measures taken against Germany to enforce her obligations under the treaty were not to be regarded as hostile acts.

FRENCH OCCUPY THE RUHR

The League, however, was stillborn. It was hampered from the outset by the refusal of the United States to participate, in spite of the fact that it owed its birth to President Wilson, who incorporated the idea in his Fourteen Points for the liquidation of the war in January, 1918. In practice, however, member nations refused to take notice of the League's dictates on matters that affected their own sovereignty or national policy.

There was no room for Germany in this new League of Nations. Not until she had paid her debts could she share in its councils.

But Germany could not pay, and the bitterness which was inevitable on both sides increased when Raymond Poincaré became Premier of France in 1922. A son of Lorraine, he hated the Germans with a loathing that was almost fanatical. He would make them pay their debts whatever the cost to the German people. Britain took a more lenient view, but Poincaré, refusing to be robbed of his prey, announced his intention of recovering France's debts at the point of the bayonet with or without the co-operation of Great Britain. In January, 1923, French troops poured into the Ruhr; 147,000 Germans were expelled from their homes; a hundred were shot in the streets; newspapers were suppressed and offices seized. Germany resisted the invasion by economic strike. The mark crashed, ruining the greater part of Germany's middle class, hunger riots spread from town to town; shops were plundered, and in the end Gustav Stresemann, who had become

Chancellor in August, realizing the futility of further resistance, called the strikes off.

New hope rose with the fall of Poincaré in 1924. A revised reparations scheme was worked out by the American politician General C. G. Dawes, chairman of the Reparations Committee. The Dawes' Plan provided for German payments of two thousand million marks per year, but did not fix the total amount. On 2 September, Germany paid the first instalment. The situation was further eased on 31 July, 1925, when the last French troops marched out of the Ruhr. In addition, Britain, U.S.A. and other countries assisted Germany's economic reconstruction with loans which between 1924 and 1930 more than offset the sum paid in reparations.

On 16 November, 1925, an event occurred which seemed to sweep the last clouds from the political sky: the Treaty of Locarno was concluded between Britain, France, Germany, Italy and Belgium. By this treaty the signatories undertook to maintain their present mutual frontiers and abstain from the use of force against each other. At the same time Germany recognized the demilitarization of the Rhineland.

The process of reconciliation having once begun proceeded apace. Early in 1926 Britain completed her evacuation of Cologne, and in September Germany took her place as a great power in the councils of the League of Nations. Disarmament was in the air, the League was in the ascendant and when, on 27 August, 1928, most of the nations of the world put their signatures to the Kellogg-Briand Pact in Paris, an international agreement by which the countries concerned undertook not to resort to war as an instrument for settling international disputes, it looked as if the spectre of war had been banished for long years to come.

LEAGUE'S FIRST SETBACK

Relations between Germany and her neighbours continued to improve. In 1930 the adoption of the Young Plan eased still further the burden of Germany's war debt, whilst the Allies' evacuation of the Rhineland, begun in 1929 and completed on 30 June, 1930, restored to Germany her full measure of self-respect.

The League received its first setback in 1931. On 18 September Japan invaded China and seized many strategic points in Manchuria. China appealed to the League and as a result Japan was ordered to evacuate the occupied territory by 16 November. She refused however and declared

Hitler becomes Chancellor

NEW CHANCELLOR SITS WITH OLD PRESIDENT. After the Presidential elections in July, 1932, Hitler demanded to be made Chancellor of the Reich. Hindenburg, who disliked the Nazis, refused, but in January of the following year he was prevailed upon to dismiss Schleicher and appoint Hitler Chancellor in his place. In the above picture the aged President is seen seated between the new Chancellor and Goering, the newly-appointed Premier of Prussia, at the commemoration of the Battle of Tannenberg in 1914.

that she would tolerate no interference. The Western powers were unwilling to do more than pass moral condemnation and the ideal of collective security was undermined. Japan continued her war and left the League.

Events in the Far East were quickly forgotten. Europe had troubles of her own far more near and more pressing than the war in China. In 1931 a terrible economic blizzard was sweeping across the world. It revealed the appalling weakness of Germany's economic status and obliged her to cease payment of reparations. Even America came perilously close to bankruptcy, and Britain was forced off the gold standard. Concerned with their own troubles the Western democracies were in no mood to take heed of what was happening to Germany or fully to appreciate its significance.

Germany was the first European country to be affected by the crisis. Production fell and unemployment rose. By the winter of 1930-31 there were already over three million unemployed. Employers began to cut wages. Under the Papen-Schleicher Government of 1932 the average weekly wage was reduced to fifty per cent of what it had been in 1929. By the winter of 1931-32 unemployment had risen to close on nine millions. In the blackness of her despair political forces which had barely been kept in check behind the façade of Social Democracy, under which Germany had been living since 1919, throve and prospered, and the doctrines of a one-time Austrian house painter, Adolf Hitler, began to echo round the land.

Hitler's political career began in earnest in 1919, when he joined the German Labour Party. He soon became its leader, and with the object of gaining the support of the genuine Socialists as well as the Nationalists, the title of the party was changed to the National Socialist German Labour Party. From the very beginning the National Socialists agitated against the Versailles Treaty and as more and more of the middle class were affected by the continuous inflation, the more popular their policy became. Hitler soon attracted

How the war began

the attention of a number of capitalists who, realizing the value of his party as a weapon against the militant sections of the working class, gave it considerable financial support.

On 9 November, 1923, Hitler attempted to seize power, but the *putsch* failed and he was sentenced to five years' detention in a fortress. Released after eight months, he reorganized the party, but the Nazis, for the moment at any rate, almost disappeared from the political arena.

HITLER BECOMES CHANCELLOR

The great economic crisis, however, gave Hitler another chance. Again backed by the industrialists, whom he promised to protect from the rising tide of Communism in Germany, Hitler won a spectacular success in the elections of 14 September, 1930, and when he stood against Hindenburg in the Presidential election of 13 March, 1932, he ran the old President so close that Hindenburg, fearing a plot to overthrow the Government, issued a decree abolishing Nazi troops. But Hitler's star was in the ascendant, and in July he demanded to be made Chancellor of the Reich. Hindenburg refused.

Now Hitler's backers came to his aid. Hoping to use him as a tool to recover their fallen fortunes, they persuaded Hindenburg to offer him the Chancellorship. Schleicher, the Chancellor, was dismissed, and on 30 January, 1933, Hitler became Chancellor of the German Reich with a mixed cabinet of Nazis and Nationalists.

Hitler was Chancellor, but full power was not in his hands. He had to eliminate all other parties from the Government if he was to become dictator of Germany. He had to act quickly for the resistance of the workers to a Hitler dictatorship was growing rapidly in all parts of the Reich, and in view of the anti-Fascist feeling Hitler's prospects at the coming election were anything but bright.

The process of elimination began with the Communist Party. Hitler launched a furious attack on the revolutionary workers through the Nazi Press, and after the Reichstag fire, on 27-28 February, he accused the Communists of the crime and used this as a pretext for arresting large numbers of his opponents and restricting their activities in the coming election. World opinion, however, was almost certainly right in naming the Nazis, not the Communists, as the real incendiaries.

Hitler raised the slogan that he had saved Germany from the horrors of a Communist uprising, but even so, he only polled forty-four per cent of the vote when the elections were held on 5 March. He managed, however, to obtain an empowering act and ruled dictatorially with the aid of his party troops, the S.A. and the S.S.

From now on Hitler had a free hand. On 6 April he took over complete control of German industry, and a fortnight later he appointed Hermann Goering, his faithful follower from the early days of the party, Premier of Prussia.

Meanwhile, the rest of Europe, wrapped in its own economic problems, took little notice of what was happening in Germany. Only a few clearsighted prophets, amongst whom was Mr. Winston Churchill, realized the full significance of Hitler's rise to power. Their warnings regarding the future peace and prosperity of Europe, however, went unheeded.

But if Hitler dealt ruthlessly with internal opposition, he was careful not to tread on the toes of the great powers. His speeches to the Western democracies were fair and soft. He talked peace and sent his representative to the disarmament conference then sitting at Geneva. It was at this conference that he showed his teeth for the first time. He demanded equality with Britain and France and a plan was put forward whereby the Allies were to disarm gradually within a period of eight years.

The conference, however, ended in a fiasco, largely because it did not provide for immediate German rearmament up to the level of the other powers, but suggested only limited German rearmament during the period of transition. On 14 October, 1933, Germany walked out of the conference, and withdrew from the League.

Hitler was now getting into his stride. Any one who even dared to criticize the new regime was flung into a concentration camp. Even members of his own party had to tread carefully, as was shown by the great purge of 30 June, 1934, when he arrested and executed a number of his most trusted adherents whom he suspected of plotting against him.

DEATH OF DOLLFUSS

In July, 1934, Hitler very nearly went too far. He ordered a Nazi uprising in Austria, with whose affairs he had promised not to interfere, hoping thereby to overthrow Chancellor Dollfuss and put Austria in Germany's pocket. Dollfuss was killed and the rising was put down by the Austrian Government whilst Mussolini, dictator of Italy, mobilized the Italian Army, and Mr. Stanley

NEW WATCH ON THE RHINE. On 7 March, 1936, Hitler struck another blow at the Treaty of Versailles and took his first step on the road of aggression. He marched his troops into the demilitarized zones of the Rhineland. Once more, on France's eastern border, stood silent figures, like these two German sentries silhouetted against the towers and chimneys of Coblenz across the river, who, from the ramparts of the historic fort of Ehrenbreitstein, maintain the ceaseless watch of Germany's historic river, the Rhine.

Baldwin, in a speech on 30 July, named the Rhine as Britain's frontier. Hitler subsequently washed his hands of this insurrection.

On 2 August, President Hindenburg died, and on the 19th, Hitler, as Fuehrer, combined the offices of President and Chancellor.

The early months of 1935 brought still further triumphs to the Fuehrer. On 13 January, after a plebiscite held under British control, the Saar territory reverted to Germany, and in March, Hitler reintroduced conscription in open defiance of the provisions of the Versailles Treaty. Still the democracies did nothing. They refused to take any action and contented themselves with ineffectual protests. Hitler took no notice, and from

that moment the rearmament of Germany, which had already begun in secret, proceeded brazenly on a scale the world had never seen before.

Hitler now concentrated all his efforts on the complete reorganization of Germany's industrial, economic and political life. He smashed the trade unions and in their place established the German Labour Front, an organization which took away from the workers their last vestige of liberty and transformed them into abject slaves of the State. Wages fell to a new low level, and hours lengthened, but his vast armament factories, his new armies and his secret police rapidly absorbed Germany's unemployed. He crushed all opposition with brutal ruthlessness. Jews, Liberals,

How the war began

Socialists, Communists suffered persecutions and tortures that horrified the world. The rubber truncheons and the concentration camps of the Gestapo, coupled with an iron censorship, robbed the German people of freedom of body and mind.

By depressing the standard of living of his people Hitler built up an astonishing degree of economic self-sufficiency. He harnessed the whole organizational genius of the country, its vast resources of labour and material, into the creation of one monstrous machine of war.

As it arose, Hitler matured his policy. At home he exploited the temperament of the German people and organized mammoth military parades. He skilfully fostered their national pride by ceaseless agitation against the injustices of the Versailles Treaty and demands for the return of German colonies and European possessions. For external consumption he worked up a campaign of hatred against Russia and set himself up as the saviour of Europe against Bolshevism.

By this means Hitler lulled the democracies into a false sense of security as Germany's armaments steadily piled up. He persuaded the people of Britain and France that war between Germany and Russia was inevitable, and under the influence of this belief the democracies were content to let events take their course, for they believed precisely what Hitler wished them to believe—that he was bent on an eastern conquest.

On 18 June, 1935, Hitler concluded a naval pact with Great Britain. This pact was the first international agreement which openly disregarded the conditions of the Treaty of Versailles. It permitted Germany to build a navy up to thirty-five per cent of the strength of the British fleet. Its conclusion was hailed as a great success in Germany, for it inaugurated a period in which Great Britain was considered a friend of the Third Reich. In the light of later events, however, it would appear to have been just another of Hitler's clever ruses to throw dust in the Allies' eyes and add conviction to the belief that it was eastwards, not to the west, that Germany's new armies would eventually march.

ANTI-COMINTERN PACT

In November, 1935, he strengthened this belief still further by concluding the Anti-Comintern Pact with Japan. The signatories undertook to inform each other of the activities of the Communist International, to consult each other on the necessary protective measures, and carry out these measures in close co-operation.

Meanwhile the international horizon had become clouded by Italy's aspirations in Africa. Obsessed with the idea of creating a new Roman Empire, Mussolini, the Italian dictator, cast covetous eyes on Abyssinia, the only independent kingdom remaining in the continent. Inevitably he excited the alarm of Britain and France, both of whom were concerned for their African possessions. Nevertheless, on 2 October, Mussolini's legions crossed the Abyssinian frontier.

CONQUEST OF ABYSSINIA

The conscience of the world was outraged, Abyssinia appealed to the League, of which she was a member, and no less than fifty nations combined to impose sanctions upon Italy. Unfortunately, these were half-hearted and limited to an incomplete economic blockade.

The campaign continued and was completed when the Italians used poison gas against the poorly-armed Abyssinian levies. By 5 May, 1936, Addis Ababa, the capital, was in Italian hands, and four days later Mussolini proclaimed the annexation of the country.

The League had failed again, and Hitler was not slow to take advantage of its failure. He had watched the democracies' feeble efforts to settle the Abyssinian affair with ill-concealed satisfaction, and on 7 March, 1936, confident that no one would raise a finger to stop him, had ordered his new troops to enter the demilitarized Rhineland, thus violating the Treaty of Locarno and dealing yet another blow at Versailles. It was a critical moment. Had Britain and France acted, Hitler would have fallen—indeed it is said that he had threatened to commit suicide if he failed—but they did not act. Divided counsels and a passionate desire for peace at any price paralysed the will of these two nations which were destined in the first place to be his dupes and later his victims.

Hitler promised not to refortify the occupied area and declared that he had no territorial demands to make in Europe, but, nevertheless, the Rhineland was the touchstone of his subsequent success and the foundation of his unbounded faith in his star. From that moment he moved steadily towards his goal of world domination.

The failure of the League over Abyssinia inevitably drove Mussolini into Hitler's arms. Hitler tempted the Italian dictator with prospects of new power and with territory, and Mussolini needed but little persuasion to throw in his lot

IMPERIAL CITY NO MORE. Hitler's programme of aggression proceeded with clockwork regularity. Made bold by his unopposed occupation of the Rhineland two years earlier, the Fuehrer, again breaking his oft-pledged word, marched his troops across the Austrian frontier on 11 March, 1938. Austria, powerless to defend herself, could do nothing. Britain and France still clung to the belief that Hitler could be placated and the peace of Europe saved. Vienna, an imperial city, which for twenty-five years had been bereft of its empire, echoed to the tramp of the Fuehrer's legions, whilst the Fuehrer, himself an Austrian, took the salute.

with Germany. The first links in the Axis chain were being forged.

These two powers moved together when the Spanish Civil War broke out on 18 July, 1936. They promised support to General Franco when he challenged the constituted legal authority of the Spanish Republican Government, and while the democracies hesitated they poured troops and war materials into the Spanish peninsula. Despite their heroism, the Spanish Republicans were overthrown and went down in ruin before the aeroplanes, tanks and " volunteers " of Hitler and Mussolini, in April, 1939.

AUSTRIA SEIZED

Meanwhile, the Continental situation had become worse. While the democracies were debating as to what, if anything, should be done in Spain, Hitler was preparing another blow. He chose his moment with consummate skill.

In the spring of 1938 he began to make new demands on Austria. Hypocritically he preached the misfortunes of the Austrian Nazis, and after a week of crisis he summoned Dollfuss's successor, Chancellor Schuschnigg, to Berchtesgaden, his mountain retreat in Bavaria, and forced him under threats of immediate invasion to sign an agreement opening up the way for Nazism in Austria. It did not matter to him that he had pledged his solemn word time after time to respect Austrian independence, for by this time the Axis was firmly established. Valiantly Schuschnigg resisted. On his return to Austria he tried to organize a plebiscite designed to furnish proof of Austria's reluctance to be absorbed by Germany, but this was forestalled by the sudden march in of German troops on the night of 11-12 March.

Again the democracies wrangled. Was this a cause for war or was it a legitimate aspiration of Germany's political existence? The latter view won and nothing was done. Hitler hastened to assure the world that he had " no further territorial claims in Europe," and authorized Goering, his right-hand man, to declare in his name that he had no intention of attacking Czechoslovakia. The Czechs, however, were alarmed, for they recalled that he had made precisely the same statement after his re-occupation of the Rhineland.

The storm was not long in breaking. Almost immediately after the seizure of Austria a violent campaign was launched in the German Press against the Czech Government under Dr. Benes. The Sudeten German movement under the leadership of Conrad Henlein was used by the Germans to stir up disorder in that country and advertise the non-existent oppression of the German minorities. On 24 April, Henlein outlined his famous eight points at Carlsbad, in which he demanded autonomy for the Sudeten areas. These demands were fostered by every means available by Dr. Goebbels, Nazi Propaganda Minister, who denounced Prague with ever-increasing vehemence, and magnified beyond all recognition minor clashes which had occurred between small bodies of Czechs and Sudeten Germans.

On 21 May, the armed invasion of Czechoslovakia seemed inevitable, and was only prevented by British and French diplomatic action and Czech mobilization. As a consequence the menace was postponed and negotiations were resumed in a more hopeful spirit. Lord Runciman was sent to Prague on a peace mission in August and succeeded in persuading the Czech Government to consent to Henlein's demands for autonomy within Czechoslovakia, but after a visit to Hitler on 2 September, Henlein suddenly altered his demand for autonomy into one for the cession of the Sudetenland to Germany.

THE CZECH CRISIS

By this time information had reached the Western capitals which left no doubt of Hitler's intention to apply force to obtain his demands, and as both France and Russia were bound by treaty to go to Czechoslovakia's aid, Britain was automatically involved since she would have to help France. Mr. Chamberlain, the British Prime Minister, therefore, took the momentous step of seeking a personal interview with the German Fuehrer, and on 15 September he flew to Berchtesgaden. The meeting resulted in an Anglo-French plan for the cession of certain purely German territories to the Reich, and a plebiscite in certain neighbouring areas. The proposal was accepted by Prague under strong pressure from the Western powers, and a second meeting between the two leaders took place at Godesberg on 23 September, when Mr. Chamberlain was able to inform Hitler that the terms discussed at their first meeting had been accepted by the Czechs. But in the meantime Hitler had increased his demands, and he put forward further proposals which were quite unacceptable. Mr. Chamberlain returned to London, convinced that war was inevitable.

At the last minute, however, he again took the initiative, and asked Mussolini to act as mediator in the dispute. Mussolini agreed, and as a result a four-power conference was held at Munich on

To GERMANY OCTOBER
To POLAND OCTOBER
To HUNGARY NOVEMBER
1938

THE MUNICH AGREEMENT. Having digested Austria, Hitler turned to Czechoslovakia. He based his claims on that country upon the alleged ill-treatment of the German minorities in the Sudetenland and began his attack by means of vigorous but wholly unscrupulous propaganda for incorporation of certain Czech areas within the Reich. Europe was on the verge of war when Mr. Chamberlain, in September, 1938, flew to Germany to negotiate with the Fuehrer. The result was the dismemberment of Czechoslovakia, shown in the map above. At top the British Premier is seen walking with Ribbentrop in Germany; below he is seen on his return to Britain at the airport, waving aloft another of Hitler's worthless pledges. He had accepted the Munich agreement as a symbol that "Britain and Germany should never go to war with each other again."

NAZIS ENTER THE CZECH CAPITAL. The policy of appeasement, which reached its climax at Munich, died overnight when, with no word of warning, Hitler marched his legions into Prague, in March, 1939. A thrill of fear ran through Europe. From that moment war was inevitable. As the Nazi troops filed into Prague's famous Hradçin Castle (above), the seat of government, welcomed only by the capitol's pro-German community, the war industries of Europe began to roar into accelerated momentum in preparation for the inevitable "Day."

29 September. There Mr. Chamberlain, M. Daladier, the French Premier, Hitler and Mussolini met and came to an arrangement which, although it dissipated the clouds of war, deprived Czechoslovakia of vast areas of her land and left her broken and impotent before the Nazi juggernaut.

Other nations shared in the spoils. Poland obtained an area in Eastern Silesia with the town of Teschen and large coal mines and steelworks, and Hungary obtained a large strip of land in Southern Slovakia and Carpathian Russia (*see* map on page 11).

The peace of Europe was saved, but for how long few people had the courage to ask. The immediate effect was a great revival of hope. Hitler had succeeded in his oft-stated ambition of absorbing a great majority of European Germans into the new Reich, but would he be content to stop there? That was a question that only the future could answer.

Hitler did not fail to make his usual declaration. This time he was more emphatic. " This is the last territorial claim I have to make in Europe," he said, " I have assured Mr. Chamberlain and I emphasize it now that when this problem is solved Germany has no more territorial problems in Europe. . . . We do not want any Czechs. . . . I shall not be interested in the Czech State any more."

THE FATE OF CZECHOSLOVAKIA

By this time France and Britain were getting wise to Hitler's methods, but even so, there were still many people who genuinely believed that peace had been saved for their lifetime. Nevertheless, Britain finally abandoned the ideal of collective security and speeded up her armament production. During the winter hope rose and confidence grew, but that confidence was utterly shattered when, on 15 March, 1939, with no word of warning and with no shred of justification Hitler marched against the now defenceless Czechoslovakia. No resistance was offered and President Hacha was forced to sign a statement placing the country under Germany's " protection." Bohemia and Moravia became protectorates of the Reich, while Slovakia was made an independent state, likewise under German " protection." The Czech Army was disbanded.

Seven days later, on 22 March, Germany presented an ultimatum to Lithuania to surrender Memel. Lithuania gave way and Memel, too, was added to the Reich.

Hitler's breach of faith aroused world-wide indignation. By seizing the whole of Czechoslovakia he had abandoned his policy of self-determination and proved conclusively that he was bent on European domination. His ambitions became apparent to the most ardent adherents of the policy of appeasement. The European situation was revolutionized overnight, but even now Britain and France could not be fully persuaded that the menace of Hitler was directed against themselves. There were many who hoped that his moves were actuated by a determination to attack Russia. Others were becoming alarmed. But no one seriously suggested that the Allies' guarantee of Czechoslovakia given at Munich should become operative.

POLAND THREATENED

The great speed up of Britain's rearmament programme which followed Hitler's latest breach of faith provided Germany with an excuse for repudiating the Anglo-German Naval Pact in April, 1939. In a speech on 14 April, Hitler declared that the foundation on which the pact was based—that Britain and Germany would not go to war with each other—was shattered by Britain's rearmament and that there was, therefore, no longer any point in adhering to its terms. Once again he had shown how little trust could be placed in his pledged word and how little value he attached to solemn agreements once they had served his purpose.

Meanwhile Mussolini, who had derived little advantage from his Axis alliance, was becoming restive. He, too, wanted fresh territories; and so, on Good Friday morning, 7 April, 1939, he invaded the little kingdom of Albania. In twenty-four hours the conquest was complete and aggression had once more triumphed.

To add to Europe's troubles Germany now began a violent campaign against Poland for the return of Danzig and the Polish Corridor. In something of a panic Britain and France offered guarantees to Poland which were accepted. Such guarantees, however, were of small use unless they could be implemented by the weight of a Russian alliance. Efforts were made during the summer of 1939 to achieve this alliance, but negotiations dragged on interminably.

In August, 1939, Hitler revealed his true object. Whilst the democracies were still negotiating with Russia he engineered the greatest political sensation of the twentieth century and signed a non-aggression pact with the Soviet Union on

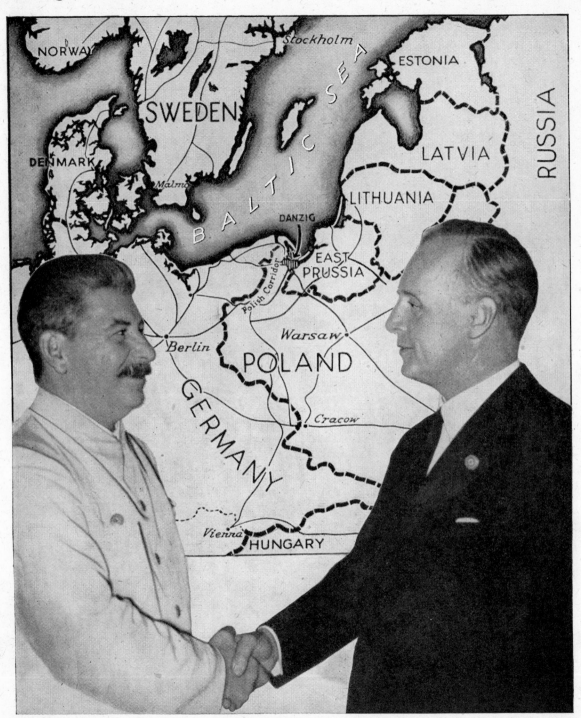

GERMAN-SOVIET PACT. The greatest political bombshell of the century burst on 23 August, when Germany and Russia signed a non-aggression pact. For years Nazis and Bolsheviks had heaped abuse on each other. War between them had seemed more certain than anything. Indeed, during the preceding months Britain and France had been trying to establish a military understanding with Moscow. This understanding was vital after the Allies had guaranteed Poland. Hitler had begun to menace Poland from the time he seized Prague. The Free City of Danzig and the Polish Corridor, seen in the above map, were made the issue. By the new pact Poland was doomed. Ribbentrop and Stalin are shaking hands after the signing of the pact in Moscow.

THE CHILDREN SENT TO SAFETY. As the war became imminent, the Government's plan for evacuating children from Britain's great towns to less vulnerable areas was put in motion. By road, rail and even sea, with gas masks, identity labels and holiday baggage, the children set off happily for what to them was a great adventure.

23 August. The rest of the world was stunned and paralysed. Poland and the peace of Europe were doomed.

Hitler, having thrown down the gauntlet, acted quickly. He backed his demands for the return of Danzig and the Polish Corridor by threats. There was little Britain and France could do to implement their guarantee, and Hitler knew it. He gambled on the belief that the Allies would not and could not go to war on the Polish issue. His demands became more urgent, and when Sir Nevile Henderson, the British Ambassador in Berlin, assured him that Britain would fulfil her obligations, and asked him to consider the dreadful responsibility that rested on his shoulders he merely replied that he was fifty years old and would prefer war now rather than when he was fifty-five or sixty.

Hitler was past caring. His non-aggression pact with Poland of 1934 meant nothing to him in 1939. He did not even trouble to specify detailed demands to Poland or to explore the possibilities of diplomacy. On 29 August he asked Poland to send a plenipotentiary to Berlin with full power to sign any agreement that should be laid before him. Poland refused and on the following day a German ultimatum was handed to the Polish Ambassador in Berlin. Before he had had time to communicate its terms to his Government Hitler announced to the world that it had been rejected and in the early dawn of Friday, 1 September, 1939, the Nazi hordes moved eastward across the Polish frontier.

Despite the valour of her armies Poland could not resist the weight of the German onslaught. She appealed to the democracies to implement their guarantees, and for two days the peace of the world hung in the balance while Britain and France solemnly reviewed the situation. And then both the democracies sent ultimatums to Hitler. Hitler took no notice and they expired on Sunday, 3 September. Britain and France were at war with Germany. The democracies had challenged the arrogance of Nazidom. On them devolved the responsibility of defending what was left of freedom, decency and right in the world.

Poland by land, sea and air

WAR BURSTS ON EASTERN EUROPE. Having signed the non-aggression pact with Russia, Hitler, confident that the Allies would not honour their pledge to Poland, launched his land, sea and air forces against that unhappy country. Here are typical scenes that followed the Nazi invasion; German bombers and infantry left in their wake burning buildings and stricken civilians. Ill-equipped Polish units fought hopelessly but gallantly to check the rapid advance of their powerful adversary.

"BRITAIN IS AT WAR WITH GERMANY"

In a broadcast from Downing Street, at 11.15 a.m. on Sunday, Sept. 3, 1939, the Prime Minister said :—

"THIS morning the British Ambassador in Berlin handed the German Government a final Note stating that unless we heard from them by eleven o'clock that they were prepared at once to withdraw their troops from Poland a state of war would exist between us.

"I have to tell you now that no such undertaking has been received, and that consequently this country is at war with Germany.

"You can imagine what a bitter blow it is to me that all my long struggle to win peace has failed. Yet I cannot believe that there is anything more, or anything different that I could have done and that would have been more successful.

"Up to the very last it would have been quite possible to have arranged a peaceful and honourable settlement between Germany and Poland, but Hitler would not have it.

"He had evidently made up his mind to attack Poland whatever happened, and although he now says he put forward reasonable proposals which were rejected by the Poles, that is not a true statement.

"The proposals were never shown to the Poles, nor to us, and though they were announced in a German broadcast on Thursday night Hitler did not wait to hear comments on them, but ordered his troops to cross the Polish frontier. His action shows convincingly that there is no chance of expecting that this man will ever give up his practice of using force to gain his will. He can only be stopped by force.

"We and France are today, in fulfilment of our obligations, going to the aid of Poland, who is so bravely resisting this wicked and unprovoked attack on her people.

"We have a clear conscience. We have done all that any country could do to establish peace.

"The situation in which no word given by Germany's ruler could be trusted and no people or country could feel themselves safe has become intolerable.

"And now that we have resolved to finish it I know that you will all play your part with calmness and courage.

"At such a moment as this the assurances of support that we have received from the Empire are a source of profound encouragement to us.

"When I have finished speaking certain detailed announcements will be made on behalf of the Government. Give these your closest attention.

"The Government have made plans under which it will be possible to carry on the work of the nation in the days of stress and strain that may be ahead. But these plans need your help.

"You may be taking your part in the fighting services or as a volunteer in one of the branches of civil defence. If so, you will report for duty in accordance with the instructions you have received.

"You may be engaged in work essential to the prosecution of war, for the maintenance of the life of the people—in factories, in transport, in public utility concerns, or in the supply of other necessaries of life.

"If so, it is of vital importance that you should carry on with your jobs.

"Now may God bless you all. May He defend the right. It is the evil things that we shall be fighting against—brute force, bad faith, injustice, oppression and persecution—and against them I am certain that the right will prevail."

11 A.M.
3RD· SEPTEMBER
1939

BRITISH ULTIMATUM EXPIRES. The British ultimatum to Germany demanding the immediate withdrawal of her troops from Poland expired at 11 a.m. on Sunday morning, 3 September, 1939. The nation, still ignorant of the fatal hour, but knowing that only a miracle could avert the death-struggle between the forces of fear and of freedom, steeled itself for the ordeal that lay before it. To the democratic governments and peoples of Britain and France fell the awful responsibility of defending the freedom of the world against Nazi domination.

WINSTON CHURCHILL AT THE ADMIRALTY. It was with an immense sense of relief that the British public learned on 3 September that Mr. Churchill had been appointed First Lord of the Admiralty. Twenty-five years earlier, in 1914, he had held the same post with outstanding success. Although Mr. Churchill had been virtually a political exile since 1929, he nevertheless had retained immense prestige with the British public. His repeated warnings of the ever-growing menace of Nazidom to the peace of Europe, had earned him the title of Nazi Enemy No. 1. Here he pauses on the steps of the Admiralty as he arrives to take up his new post.

S.S. " ATHENIA " TORPEDOED. Within a few hours of the outbreak of war a German U-boat claimed its first victim. With no warning, the liner " Athenia," bound from Belfast to Montreal with over 1,000 passengers many of whom were women and children, was torpedoed in the Atlantic. All but 112 were fortunately picked up by ships which hurried to her assistance. As a number of the passengers were Americans, the German propaganda department put out the ridiculous story that a British submarine, on Mr. Churchill's orders, had committed the deed in order to influence American opinion. The " Athenia " is seen settling down by the stern.

WAR COMES TO BRITAIN. Anxious faces lined the pavement in Downing Street on that fine Sunday morning as Mr. Chamberlain, in the Cabinet Room of No. 10, began his broadcast. Almost as he finished speaking the wail of air raid sirens all over the country electrified the already tense atmosphere. Londoners, expecting bombs to drop, made their way into the shelters in quiet and orderly groups. It was a false alarm, and soon the sirens sounded the "raiders passed" signal, but no declaration of war could have been more dramatic.

The Empire stands by Britain

THE EMPIRE'S CALL TO ARMS. Dominions, colonies, every partner in the Empire rallied to " stand with Britain " at the outbreak of war. The representative impressions (above) of the men, the guns, the ships and the planes with which Australia, Canada, New Zealand, South Africa, India and their fellow countries prepared to take part in the struggle, is a fit symbol of the steadfast purpose of a united Commonwealth of free peoples, determined not to sheathe the sword until the world is free once and for all from the threat of Nazi tyranny.

THE " AUSSIES " GET GOING.   Australia, planning for an army of 200,000 trained men by summer 1940, had already by the beginning of October, 1939, a first draft of 40,000 militia in camp for training.   Above are seen some of the Commonwealth's new forces waiting with their baggage to make their first acquaintance with the inside of a training camp, and, a little later, ready to embark for the Near East and the Motherland in fulfilment of the promise of their Premier, Mr. R. G. Menzies, on 2 September, that "We stand with Britain."

India answers the call

INDIA'S PART IN THE WAR. Although the All-India Congress Party would not identify itself actively with the Empire's war effort after the Viceroy's declaration of the postponement of further steps towards granting the country Dominion status, in the first few weeks over 200 ruling princes affirmed their loyalty to the British Raj, many with offers of immediate help. The pictures show: above, a sentry guarding a railway bridge in Northern India; below, Indian Army recruits taking a geography lesson at their open air training school.

GERMAN ARTILLERY MOVES UP. To economize their stocks of petrol the Germans used thousands of horse-drawn vehicles to follow up the advance of their mechanized units during the Polish campaign. Here a German gun team, crossing a river by one of the few intact bridges, seems to be finding the Polish road, churned up by their own tanks and armoured cars, difficult to negotiate.

POLISH INFANTRY ATTACKING. In spite of their great fighting qualities and powers of endurance, the Polish Army could do little to check the swift advance of the enemy's armoured columns. Nevertheless they faced with courage a tremendously superior enemy in an heroic attempt to defend their homeland. The picture shows Polish infantry charging forward to the attack.

27

BRITISH BOMBERS OVER WILHELMSHAVEN. The first great air raid of the war was launched on 4 September against enemy warships in the Wilhelmshaven and Kiel areas. The "Wellington" bombers that took part faced most difficult weather conditions, but the attack was resolutely pressed home in face of severe fire from enemy

ground defences and naval units. This reconstruction of the raid, specially drawn by Edgar Thurstan, shows an attack by a flight of British machines on a German pocket battleship in the Schilling Roads. The planes descended to within a hundred feet of the sea and scored a direct hit. No bombs were dropped on land.

POLISH FORTRESS BATTERED INTO SUBMISSION.
For six days and nights the 11-inch guns of the German battleship "Schleswig-Holstein" bombarded the Polish fort of Westerplatte, on the outskirts of Danzig, at point-blank range (right) whilst from the land and air furious assaults were made by large and well-equipped German forces. For six days the Poles held out, but on the seventh the gallant commander of the tiny garrison surrendered to save what were left of his men. It was estimated that the German land forces alone amounted to a division, whereas the defenders, all told, numbered only a company. The picture above shows the Nazi flag being hoisted by German soldiers over the shell-torn battlements after the garrison surrendered.

Fort Westerplatte strikes its colours

B.E.F. LANDS IN FRANCE. The plans for the transportation of men and material to France had been drawn up by the French and British General Staffs long before the war clouds broke, so that when war was declared it only remained to put them into operation. With great speed—and even greater secrecy—men, guns, tanks and all the equipment and supplies necessary to maintain an army in the field, were shipped across the Channel, and it was not until 12 September, by which time most of the material had safely arrived, that the British public were let into the secret. The picture on the right shows troops and guns being disembarked at a French port. Above is seen Viscount Gort, V.C., who was appointed Commander-in-Chief of the British armies in France, under the supreme command of General Gamelin.

British Official Photograph: Crown Copyright Reserved.

NAVY'S FIRST BIG WARTIME LOSS. H.M. Aircraft Carrier "Courageous" was struck amidships by a torpedo from a German submarine whilst on patrol on 17 September, and sank within a very short time. Orders to abandon ship were given five minutes after she was struck, but her gallant commander, Captain Mackeig-Jones

Torpedoing of H.M. Aircraft Carrier "Courageous"

(in circle) remained on the bridge to the end and went down with his ship. The picture shows the "Courageous" heeling over shortly before her death plunge; her crew can be clearly seen scrambling down the side into the water. The "Courageous" had a full complement of 1,126 officers and men, of whom 515 lost their lives.

HORRORS OF INVADED POLAND. The horrors of modern aerial warfare are forcefully illustrated by this picture of a little Warsaw boy squatting miserably among the wreckage of what was his home. Scenes such as this were common all over Poland where Goering's air force rained death and destruction on countless open towns and brought untold misery and hardship to Poland's civilian population. In spite of constant raids, however, and the indiscriminate damage they wrought, the morale of Poland's civilians remained unshaken to the end.

Nazis leave desolation in their wake

GERMAN ADVANCE IN POLAND. Simultaneously from four sides Hitler's forces marched towards Warsaw, and as the endless lines of vehicles made their way through the countryside, villages (as in the picture above) and farmsteads (below) were reduced to shapeless heaps of rubble. The Poles hoped in vain that the autumn rains would hold up the onrush, but their hopes were mocked by cloudless skies, and the occupation of Western Poland, for which Hitler's time-table had allowed a month, took little over a week.

DESTROYER RESCUES NAZI AIRMEN. From the early days of the war German seaplanes based on Sylt carried out reconnaissance flights to Britain and attacked merchant shipping with bombs and machine guns. The Navy and the R.A.F. took steady toll of these marauders. Above a British destroyer is seen approaching a Nazi seaplane shot down off the coast. Right, the German airmen are preparing to launch their collapsible rubber boat. The Navy saved the lives of scores of Nazi airmen.

Last hours of Warsaw's resistance

GERMAN TROOPS FIGHTING IN WARSAW'S SUBURBS. Masses of mechanized forces, hundreds of bombing planes, working together in close co-operation, were the primary reason for German successes in Poland. Yet, despite the Poles' enormous inferiority in both these arms, it was a month before the Germans forced the capital to surrender. These two pictures illustrate the final phase of Warsaw's resistance. Above, German artillery, powerfully supported by tanks, is seen battering its way through the streets on the outskirts of the city. Below, infantry are advancing along a tram-blocked street behind the cover of light tanks.

WARSAW'S RESISTANCE ENDS. On 15 September the Germans claimed to have surrounded Warsaw, but it was not until the 27th that the capital, battered by aerial and artillery bombardment, was forced to capitulate. On that day, high officers of the Polish and German armies met in a bus on the outskirts of the capital

Polish garrison leaves the devastated city

and arranged terms of surrender (in circle) Three days later the remnants of the heroic Polish garrison marched out of the city, which was occupied by Nazi forces.   The above picture shows the disarmed soldiers marching dejectedly out of the capital they had so bravely defended, watched by the civilian population.

BOMBED POLISH ARMOURED TRAIN. This remarkable picture shows what happened to a Polish armoured train attacked by a Nazi bomber. High explosive bombs weighing 520 lb. were used in the attack; their destructive effect can be gathered from the damage to the train itself as well as from the size of the bomb crater.

Germany and Russia share the spoils

A NEW DIVISION OF POLAND.

Yet again unhappy Poland was divided amongst her neighbours when on 29 September Ribbentrop in Moscow signed a second Soviet-German agreement defining the boundaries of the German and Soviet occupied areas of the country. The map (right) shows how the territory was divided. Above, Molotov, Russian Premier, signs the agreement on behalf of the Soviets. Behind him stand Ribbentrop and Stalin. Germany took not only Danzig and the Polish Corridor, but Warsaw and vast areas to the south which had never had any German population. Russia limited her claims to the area east of Brest-Litovsk, an area predominantly Ukrainian, and almost identical with that bounded by the famous "Curzon Line." This line had been suggested as the frontier between Poland and Russia by Lord Curzon in 1920. Germany secured all the coal mines and the heavy industrial areas, while Russia obtained the rich oilfields of Galicia.

NAZI CONQUERORS IN SILENT WARSAW. On 5 October Hitler flew to Warsaw to take the salute at the march past of his victorious troops. The route was carefully chosen to avoid those parts of the city that had been devastated by aerial bombardment, and the streets were lined by Nazi troops to keep the crowds in check. This precaution, however, seemed unnecessary since Warsaw's population stayed indoors, and the procession made its way through almost deserted streets, as can be seen from the above picture.

Hitler launches his peace offensive

HITLER MAKES HIS " PEACE " SPEECH IN THE REICHSTAG. At the conclusion of his Polish campaign Hitler addressed the Reichstag on the European situation, and made suggestions for the cessation of hostilities and for settling problems resulting from the war. Mr. Chamberlain and M. Daladier, replying a few days later, rejected his overtures, and refused to enter into negotiations with the German Government on the grounds that no lasting peace could be made until Hitler had clearly shown that his word could be trusted.

FRENCH AND GERMAN PATROLS AT WORK. Although during the first few months of the war there were no large scale operations on the Western Front, patrols from both sides were constantly seeking information concerning the strength and disposition of the opposing forces.   Above, a French patrol moves cautiously through a shell-torn village, whilst (below) Germans are seen engaged on a similar errand.

"ROYAL OAK" TORPEDOED. By a feat of great daring and skill, to which Mr. Churchill himself paid tribute, a German U-boat, under the command of Lieutenant Prien, penetrated the defences of Scapa Flow and torpedoed the British battleship H.M.S. "Royal Oak" on 14 October. "It appears probable," said Mr. Churchill, speaking to the House of Commons on 17 October, "that the U-boat fired a salvo of torpedoes of which only one hit the bow. Twenty minutes later the U-boat fired three or four torpedoes, and these, striking in quick succession, caused the ship to capsize and sink." The "Royal Oak," a ship of 29,000 tons, had a main armament of eight 15-in. guns. Eight hundred and ten British seamen lost their lives. Germany acclaimed it as a triumph, and Prien and his crew were given a well-staged reception in Berlin on their return as seen in the above picture.

RAID ON THE FIRTH OF FORTH. On 16 October an ineffective attack was launched by German warplanes upon British warships in the Firth of Forth. The above photograph, taken from one of the enemy machines, was published upside down in a Berlin illustrated paper, and purported to show a bomb bursting on the bridge. The "bomb explosion," which can be seen just to the left of the centre pier, is, in reality, Inch Garvie Island upon which the pier is built. Although the raid was carried out by twelve or fourteen

British warships in the Firth of Forth

enemy bombers only very slight damage was done to three British ships, the cruisers "Southampton" and "Edinburgh," and the destroyer "Mohawk." German aircraft had flown over Rosyth to reconnoitre earlier in the morning, and the first of the series of actual raids began about 2.30 in the afternoon and continued until 4 p.m., when the last of the German planes was chased away by R.A.F. fighters. Only two civilian casualties were reported and the railway continued its normal service over the bridge uninterruptedly. Four enemy planes were brought down. The picture above shows an enemy plane being driven off by anti-aircraft fire after dropping a bomb near H.M.S. "Edinburgh." On the right is the funeral of two of the Nazi airmen killed in the raid.

U.S. SENATE REPEALS EMBARGO. On 27 October, after more than a month of fierce debate, the U.S. Senate voted for the repeal of the embargo on war materials that formed a part of America's Neutrality Law. This meant that belligerent countries could purchase war materials from the U.S. only if they paid for them in cash and carried them in their own ships. Above, President Roosevelt is seen making his celebrated speech to Congress when he urged the repeal of the embargo. The effect of repeal was to place U.S.A. war production at the disposal of the Allies; the British blockade precluded Germany from buying in America.

New Zealand trains her own pilots

NEW ZEALAND IN ARMS. New Zealand declared war on Germany on 3 September. Volunteers at once rushed to join up in the land and air forces, and some six hundred New Zealand residents in, or visitors to, London, immediately registered for service, many of them joining a special New Zealand anti-tank unit. At the outbreak of war, besides its own Home Defence Air Force, the Dominion had four hundred pilots trained or training in England with the British R.A.F., and other trainees completed their course in Canada. The picture above shows a flight of " Avro " training planes from New Zealand's own Air Force school at Wigram out on a practice flight.

AUSTRALIA'S FLEET STANDS BY. Australia's Navy, which dates from 1911, a small but highly efficient force, worked during the peace years in close co-operation with the British Navy, with which officers and personnel were regularly interchanged. Above, the 8-in. guns of the 10,000-ton cruiser " Canberra," flagship of the Commonwealth squadron, are seen firing a salvo during manœuvres at Jervis Bay, New South Wales. Below, Australia's second largest ship, the 6,830-ton cruiser " Sydney." Not only at sea was Australia

Force ready for action

prepared for immediate action. Her Air Force, too, though small, was highly trained and it was soon realized that the Dominion could make a useful contribution to the war effort in the air. In October, 1939, a scheme was announced under which personnel from all parts of the Commonwealth would be trained in Canada, and the Dominion began producing machines at speed. Above, three "Wirraway" planes, Australian built after an adaptation of an American design. Below, Australian cadets from the Richmond training school.

CANADA'S SHARE IN THE WAR. A special session of Parliament was called on 7 September to decide Canada's war policy, and the Dominion declared war three days later. Canada's central situation in the Empire, her possession of an important aircraft industry that could readily expand, and her wealth of raw material, dictated the choice of the Dominion as a central Imperial air base, and she undertook responsibility for supervising the training of the air personnel from other Dominions as provided by the Empire Air Scheme. Steps were at once taken to raise an expeditionary force; first expectations were that 20,000 men could be

ready to fight with Britain

trained and equipped for overseas service by early 1940, but actually Canada's first contingent of troops arrived in Britain on 17 December, 1939. The Canadian fleet of six destroyers and a small number of minesweepers was rapidly added to by purchase and new building. The pictures show: (top left) a group of twenty-seven newly-trained air pilots receiving their "wings" at Canada's key aerodrome, Trenton; (bottom left) Lord Tweedsmuir, Governor-General at the outbreak of war, chatting with a pilot at a training base; (right) one of many powerful anti-aircraft units taking part in regular defence exercises near the Canadian coast.

SOUTH AFRICA TAKES UP ARMS. Germany had hoped that racial jealousies would secure South Africa's neutrality, but the Premier, General Hertzog, who favoured this course, was unable to carry a majority of his Cabinet with him, and resigned to be succeeded by General Smuts (seen above inspecting Union troops at Johannesburg), who formed a new Government pledged to support Britain. This policy was heartily endorsed by the Union Parliament and the country, and forces were immediately embodied for service " anywhere in Africa "; some of them (below) are off in convoy to their defence stations in East Africa.

Bermuda mans her defences

A UNITED EMPIRE. Assurances of support for the Imperial Government rained in from every constituent of the Empire in the early weeks of the war. Though unable to compete with the great Dominions in sending large contingents of troops to Europe, governors of colonies and protectorates in Asia, Africa, the West Indies, and the South Seas; Moslem rulers such as the Emir of Transjordania and the Sultan of Zanzibar; chiefs of negro protectorates and native rulers of British islands in the Pacific vied in offering help. Among those who manned their own defences was little Bermuda, part of whose coastal defence is illustrated above.

MUNICH BOMB EXPLOSION. On 8 November, Hitler unexpectedly decided to attend a meeting held in the Buergerbraukeller, a beer hall in Munich, to celebrate the anniversary of the Nazi putsch of 1923. After making a violently anti-British speech, he left the building at 9.15 p.m. together with all the more important of the Nazi personalities who had accompanied him. Twenty minutes later a bomb, which had been concealed in one of the supporting pillars, shattered the edifice, causing the ceiling to collapse on the assembly, which included

Bomb explosion in the Buergerbraukeller in Munich

many of Hitler's earliest supporters. Nine people were killed, and over sixty injured. The German authorities accused the British Secret Service of responsibility for the outrage; large rewards were offered for information, and workmen who had prepared the hall, and others, arrested; but whether this was a genuine attempt on the Fuehrer's life, or just another manœuvre to increase his popularity, we may never know. Hitler is seen speaking shortly before he left the hall (left) and some of the damage done by the bomb is seen on the right.

SINKING OF THE " RAWALPINDI." On 23 November the British armed merchant cruiser, "Rawalpindi,"
a former P. and O. liner, cruising off the south of Iceland on contraband control duties as part of the Northern
Patrol, sighted the German pocket battleship "Deutschland." Her attempt at escape under cover of a smoke
screen was foiled by the approach of a second enemy ship. Signalled by the "Deutschland" to stop, the
"Rawalpindi" replied with the fire of all her starboard guns, but the bridge and wireless room were demolished

"Rawalpindi" goes down with colours flying

by the "Deutschland's" fourth shot; under the heavy fire of the two German ships the whole vessel, except the forecastle, soon became a mass of flames, and her few still undamaged boats were lowered. After a magnificent fight, the blazing wreck of the gallant "Rawalpindi" went down with colours flying, with her commanding officer Captain Kennedy, and almost all her hands, mostly merchant seamen and naval reservists. The enemy ships hurriedly withdrew from the scene on the approach of a British cruiser, but eleven survivors only were picked up.

AIR AID FROM AMERICA. The repeal of America's Neutrality Law at the end of October enabled the Allies to order aircraft from American firms, and on the very day that the Bill for repeal was signed orders amounting to £44 millions for planes and equipment were confirmed. Above, reconnaissance bombers from the Lockheed Company's California factory receiving final touches. Below, a naval dive bomber being towed across the border into Canada, as American neutrality regulations required, for shipment thence to Britain.

The Navy takes toll of U-boats

END OF A GERMAN SUBMARINE. Despite Germany's best efforts her U-boats were never able to repeat the successes they enjoyed in the last war. New methods of detection enabled the Navy to take a steady toll of the underwater raiders. In the early months Germany lost an average of three submarines a week. Most were lost without trace, but in some cases the Navy were able to rescue the crews. These pictures show a U-boat forced to the surface by depth charges (above) and boats picking up survivors (below).

RUSSIA DECLARES WAR ON FINLAND. After consolidating her gains in Poland, Russia, for strategic reasons, made certain territorial demands on Finland, and when these were refused, launched her army and air force against that tiny country. Bombs fell on Helsinki and other towns on the first day, and a pitiful stream of refugees fled across the frontier into Sweden. The pathetic picture above shows a sorrowing Finnish mother with her children taking a last look at her homeland before the train bears them into exile.

Rain of death on Finland's capital

BOMBING OF HELSINKI. Although most of the Russian air raids on Finland were directed against military objectives, it was inevitable that some of the bombs should miss their mark and inflict injury upon civilians and civilian property. Nevertheless, considering the number of bombs dropped, Finnish civilian casualties were surprisingly small. This was largely due to the efficiency of the Finnish A.R.P. Above is seen a block of flats in Helsinki which has been hit by a high explosive bomb and is blazing furiously.

W.I.P.—C

THE " WATUSSI " INTERCEPTED.   On 2 December the German passenger liner " Watussi " was intercepted off Cape Point by three South African Defence Force bombers.   She ignored an order to heave to until **two** bombs were dropped ahead of her; her captain then gave orders to scuttle her, and she sank in flames.   All her passengers and crew, who had taken to the boats, were saved.   Above is seen a South African coast patrol of converted air liners.   Below, the " Watussi," ablaze from stem to stern, just before she foundered.

A VICTIM OF THE "ADMIRAL GRAF SPEE." Before the German commerce-raiding battleship was brought to book by the British Navy, she inflicted considerable loss to merchant shipping in the South Atlantic, the largest of her nine British victims being the 10,000-ton merchantman "Doric Star" captured and torpedoed on 4 December. The picture shows an unnamed ship that met a similar fate being watched by the crew from the decks of the "Admiral Graf Spee" as she heeled over preparatory to taking her death plunge.

First great naval battle of the war:

"Graf Spee" seeks refuge in Montevideo Harbour

BATTLE OF THE RIVER PLATE. On Wednesday, 13 December, a British squadron of three light cruisers, "Exeter," "Ajax" and "Achilles," commanded by Commodore Henry Harwood, was on patrol near the mouth of the River Plate. About 6 a.m. a German vessel was sighted and the British ships immediately attacked. It proved to be the German pocket battleship "Admiral Graf Spee" which had been preying on Allied shipping in those waters. She immediately opened fire on the "Exeter," and after one or two ineffectual salvos scored a direct hit. She concentrated another turret on the "Ajax" and "Achilles," but so skilfully were they manoeuvred that they managed to keep out of harm's way. Before long the "Exeter" was reduced to one gun and forced to withdraw from the action. Although the German ship's armament was half as much again as the combined broadsides of the three British cruisers, "Ajax" and "Achilles," using incredibly daring tactics, harried their more powerful opponent with such effect that she was forced to seek refuge in Montevideo Harbour in a damaged condition. Bottom left, "Ajax" seen from "Achilles" as she attacks; the smoke on the horizon marks the position of the German ship. Above, the "Graf Spee" is seen in Montevideo Harbour after the fight. Top left, the shell-scarred bows of the "Graf Spee."

BURNING WRECK OF THE "GRAF SPEE." By international law a belligerent warship in time of war may not stay in a neutral port for more than a specified time, and the whole world waited expectantly for the "Graf Spee" to come out of Montevideo and join battle again. Outside, the British ships lay in wait, anxious to finish the job they had so well begun. But it was not to be. On the evening of 17 December, the "Graf Spee" steamed out of the harbour, but not, as was expected, to seaward, where the British ships lay in wait, but towards the west. Shortly after 8 p.m. two explosions shook the air and a flash of flame leapt skyward. The ship was blotted from

The pocket battleship "Graf Spee" scuttled by Hitler's orders

view by a dense cloud of black smoke as she crumpled up, a mass of twisted steel. She had been scuttled by her commander on express orders from Hitler. Such was the inglorious end of one of the proudest ships of the German Navy. For his brilliant conduct of the battle Commodore Harwood (in circle left) received the K.C.B. and was promoted to rear-admiral. Captain Langsdorff (in circle right), the "Graf Spee's" commander, could not endure his shame; he died by his own hand two days after he had scuttled his ship. The picture above shows the blazing wreckage of the pocket battleship a short time after the charges had been fired.

MINESWEEPERS FROM NEWFOUNDLAND. As wider and wider stretches of the North Sea and other home waters were sown with mines by the enemy more and more brave men were called for to assist in the dangerous task of clearing the seas. In December a large number of fishermen from Britain's oldest dominion, eager to help their English comrades who had volunteered for the work, arrived at a home port. Above they are cheering Rear-Admiral Bromley, who welcomed them on behalf of the Colonial Secretary.

Outposts of Empire prepare

ASIA AND AFRICA AWAIT THE SIGNAL. The outbreak of hostilities found well-trained and equipped native forces in many of the smaller British possessions on the alert and eager to play their part, in co-operation with British troops, in the cause of liberty. Above left, tribesmen of the Aden Protectorate levies, with a British officer, on the march. Right, sturdy ratings of the Nigerian Marine Department, with their white officers, at Lagos. Below, armoured carriers at manœuvres over the rough mountainous roads of Hong Kong.

"COLUMBUS" IN FLAMES. After being intercepted by a British warship about three hundred miles off the coast of Virginia on 19 December, the liner "Columbus," the third largest, and one of the most luxurious vessels in the German merchant fleet, was set on fire by her crew to avoid capture. She belonged to the North-German Lloyd line and her loss made a deep impression abroad. In the top picture she is seen blazing furiously from stem to stern. Below, her crew are seen taking to the boats.

Airmen from "down under"

A REVISED EMPIRE AIR SCHEME. A modification of the Empire Air Scheme in the late autumn of 1939 provided that Australia should train most of her own air personnel not in Canada but at home with the aid of instructors borrowed from Britain. The Commonwealth's new plan budgeted for a contribution of 26,000 trained men to the Empire Air Forces within three years. On 26 December a first Australian air contingent landed in England. The picture shows them disembarking at a south coast port.

INDIANS AND CYPRIOTS ARRIVE IN FRANCE. Political controversy over "Dominion status" did not prevent the material expression of the overwhelming desire of the Indian people to take an active part in the struggle for freedom. Detachments of the Indian Army Service Corps, still a mainly unmechanized force, began to arrive in France at the end of 1939, where their columns of pack and draught mules afforded a valuable supplement to motor transport. The picture shows some of the drivers in camp in France.

and Cyprus join the B.E.F. on the Western Front

One of the earliest of the smaller units of the Commonwealth to come forward with offers of help to the Motherland in her struggle was Cyprus, Britain's very loyal outpost in the Eastern Mediterranean. From the very beginning of hostilities recruits flocked to join the Cyprus R.A.S.C., and by the turn of the year a contingent of them had arrived in France with their mules (above) ready to assist in the transport of stores and similar duties with the various units of the B.E.F. (*British Official Photograph: Crown Coyright Reserved*)

CANADA'S AIRMEN ARRIVE.   Canadian Air Force personnel made their first landings in Britain in the last fortnight of December, as an advance guard to prepare camps and training aerodromes for the far larger number to follow—for in the last few months of 1939 seven thousand recruits, Canadian and American, had applied to join the Royal Canadian Air Force.   The airmen in the picture, fresh from a training course in Canada, have just stepped ashore, and are acknowledging the rousing welcome they found awaiting them in the Old Country.

Finnish ski-patrols active

ON THE FINNISH NORTHERN FRONT. One of the outstanding features of the Russo-Finnish War was the skill and audacity shown by the Finnish ski detachments (top). Each man was a master of the sport which had become an important wartime method of progression, and their agility and swiftness enabled them to penetrate far behind the enemy lines and harass their communications. The fearful cold in which the opposing armies had to fight is well illustrated by the frozen Russian corpses seen in the bottom picture.

BATTLE OF SUOMUSSALMI. In an attempt to cut Finland's waistline and thereby separate the Finnisn southern and northern armies, the Russians made two separate thrusts in the direction of the town of Suomussalmi, on Lake Kianta. The Finns had only one division on that front, and had at all costs to prevent the two enemy divisions from uniting. They split their forces into two, one section holding up the advance of the Russian 44th Division from the south, whilst the other fell on the Russian 163rd Division, to the north,

and annihilated it after cutting its supply lines. The Finnish forces then reunited and fell upon the Russian 44th Division, winning the greatest victory of the war on 8 January. The intense winter cold and snow was their ally, and the Russian losses in men and material were enormous. More than a thousand prisoners were taken as well as immense quantities of war material, including tanks and armoured cars. The picture shows only a small part of the havoc wrought in their transport after the Russian resistance broke.

CONVOY SYSTEM AT WORK. Experience gained in the war of 1914-18 proved conclusively that the submarine menace to shipping was considerably reduced when merchantmen travelled together in large numbers with an escort of warships. Consequently, when war broke out in September, 1939, this system

was immediately put into operation. That it was a success is proved by figures issued by the Admiralty in January, 1940, which stated that only twelve out of 5,911 British and neutral ships were sunk by enemy action whilst in convoy. This picture shows a fleet of merchantmen travelling together in convoy.

LOSS OF H.M.S. "GRENVILLE." On 21 January, H.M. destroyer "Grenville" was sunk by mine or torpedo in the North Sea. There was no time to lower the boats, but other ships in the vicinity were able to rescue most of the crew. Altogether eight men were killed by the explosion, and seventy-three were reported missing and presumed dead. These two pictures show (top) the "Grenville" just before she took her final plunge; (below) a dramatic photograph of A.B. Bromfield, the last man to leave the ship, clinging to a porthole in the bows. "Grenville," a vessel of 1,485 tons, had a complement of 175 officers and men.

BIG GERMAN GUN IN ACTION. Although during the first few months of the war there was no large-scale activity on the Western Front, there were occasional artillery outbursts on both sides designed to draw the enemy fire and thereby give some indication of the artillery strength of the forces in the opposite sector. The Germans used a number of big guns on railway mountings such as that seen firing in the picture above. Their advantage was that they could be moved rapidly from one sector to another. Most of the fighting at this period took place in the Saar-Moselle region, south-east of the Luxembourg-France border.

ROYALTY WITH THE CANADIAN ARMY. The first two contingents of troops from Canada, convoyed across the Atlantic by British warships, arrived in England on 17 December, accompanied by their Commander-in-Chief, Major-General McNaughton, who described them as "a broad cross-section of the Canadian people." They were visited in camp on 24 January by the King and Queen, who are seen (above) being welcomed by General McNaughton, and (below) discussing with a gunner "how it works." *(Canadian Military Photograph)*

Anzacs disembark at Suez

MR. EDEN WITH THE ANZACS. On 12 February the first contingent of troops from Australia and New Zealand arrived at Suez. Mr. Anthony Eden, then Secretary for the Dominions, flew to Egypt bearing messages of welcome from the King. He is here seen addressing New Zealand Troops on the crowded deck of one of the transports where he was received with enthusiasm. " They are going to be as good," said Mr. Eden on his return to England on 19 February, " as their fathers and brothers twenty-five years ago."

SHELL-SCARRED " EXETER " COMES HOME. Bearing the scars of her encounter with the German pocket battleship, "Admiral Graf Spee" (see pages 68-71) off the River Plate, H.M.S. "Exeter" steamed into Plymouth, her home port, on 15 February. She thus disproved the lie circulated widely by the Nazi propaganda department that she had been so badly damaged that she had had to be run aground to save her from sinking. The damage to her sides and funnels, although patched up and painted over, can be clearly seen.

RUSSIAN BOMBS FIRE PETROL STORE. The war in Finland continued in terrible weather with snow and bitter cold. Despite these conditions Russia's vast air force was very active bombing centres of Finnish resistance and supply depots. In the middle of February extensive raids were carried out on Aabo, an oil depot. In one of these raids a direct hit was scored. The Finns displayed great heroism in rolling out oil barrels from the blazing inferno. The picture illustrates the calmness with which they worked.

ALTMARK

THE "ALTMARK" INCIDENT. During the early days of February the German tanker "Altmark," which had acted as a supply ship to the ill-fated "Graf Spee," was nearing the end of her perilous voyage back to Germany. On board she had 300 British seamen who had been captured from ships sunk by the "Graf Spee." The British Admiralty decided that these men should be rescued and ordered the destroyer "Cossack" (Captain Vian) to intercept the German ship. With the aid of aerial reconnaissance she was located and her position was wire-lessed to the "Cossack," which intercepted her on the night of 17 February, as she was steaming down the

Norwegian coast. When the "Altmark" saw the British destroyer she sought shelter in Joessing Fjord. In spite of the fact that she was in Norwegian territorial waters, "Cossack" followed her in, ran alongside, and boarded her. In the ensuing hand-to-hand fight seven of the German crew were killed but the British seamen were released. They had been under hatches in circumstances of terrible suffering for many weeks. The captain of the "Altmark" had a fanatical hatred of anything English and his prisoners had suffered in consequence. The reconstruction above specially drawn by Edgar Thurstan shows the British sailors boarding the "Altmark."

H.M.S. " COSSACK " RETURNS WITH " ALTMARK " PRISONERS. After her gallant and successful expedition H.M.S. "Cossack" returned to Britain with the British seamen she had rescued from the Nazi prison ship, the "Altmark." The "Cossack" is seen here approaching the quayside of a Scottish port on her return, her decks packed by her crew and the seamen she had rescued. An immense crowd had assembled on the quayside to witness her triumphant return, and gave her a tumultuous welcome.

ANZACS IN THE NEAR EAST. On 12 February the first contingents of Australian and New Zealand troops arrived at Suez, to take up their war stations for the defence of Palestine, Egypt and the Near East, and were welcomed in the King's name by the Dominions Secretary, Mr. Anthony Eden (see page 87). The model town seen above, with its neatly planned rows of tents and hutments, was erected on the edge of the desert for the reception of the Anzacs, largely by native labour, in the amazingly short space of three weeks.

" GRAF SPEE " HEROES MARCH TO THE CITY. On 23 February, London gave a tumultuous welcome to the officers and men of the two British cruisers "Ajax" and "Exeter," victors of the battle against the German pocket battleship, "Admiral Graf Spee," off the River Plate in December, 1939 (see pages 68-71). There was first a royal investiture at the Horse Guards Parade at which Rear-Admiral Harwood of "Exeter" received the K.C.B. and

other officers, petty officers and men who had shared in the action were decorated. Afterwards the men marched to the City where a ceremonial luncheon was given in their honour at the Guildhall, and the Lord Mayor, Mr. Churchill and others paid tribute to the Navy's latest exploit. In the above picture the procession is seen marching through the Admiralty Arch between packed ranks of cheering Londoners on its way to the City banquet.

95

H.M.S. "Achilles" welcomed at Auckland 23 February, 1940

NEW ZEALAND SAILORS HOME. New Zealand had a rousing welcome ready for her naval heroes when H.M.S. "Achilles" visited Auckland on 23 February. As a unit of the New Zealand division, the cruiser had flown the Dominion's flag beside the white ensign at the Battle of the Plate, and 380 members of Captain Parry's gallant crew came from New Zealand. "Achilles'" deadly fire, unswerving as the "Graf Spee's" shells dropped all around her, had helped to speed the inglorious foe on her quest for safety.

ANZACS PREPARE. Through the early months of 1940 Australia was preparing a force that should carry on the glorious traditions established by the heroes of the war of 1914-18. So thorough was their preliminary work at home that little was left for them to learn from the intensive training they later received at Suez and in Britain. Above, men of the Australian Expeditionary Force, shortly to leave for the Near East to defend the Suez Canal against any attack from the west, march through Martin Place, Sydney, cheered by enormous crowds.

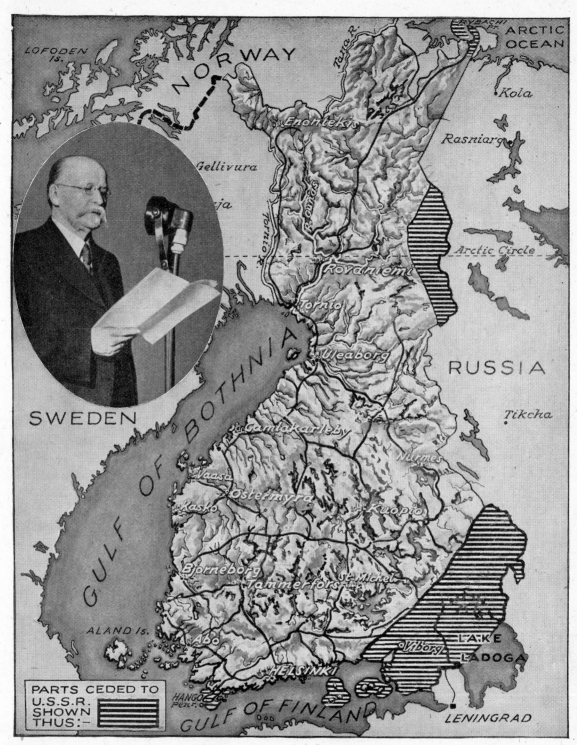

RUSSIA AND FINLAND MAKE PEACE. For 104 days the Finns stood up to the enormous power of the Red Army. Then with their Mannerheim Line irretrievably breached they made peace. The terms differed from those offered by Russia before hostilities began chiefly in that no Russian territory was ceded in return for that seized. As seen on this map, Finland ceded the whole Karelian Isthmus, an area in Central Finland and part of the Rybachi Peninsula. (Inset) President Kallio is seen broadcasting the terms to the Finnish nation.

Finns evacuate their Gibraltar

FINNS AND RUSSIANS MEET AT HANGOE. Besides losing Viborg, her most important port, Finland was forced to lease to Russia the peninsula of Hangoe, key to the Gulf of Finland. The lease was to run for thirty years at a yearly rent of about £30,000. The evacuation of the ceded areas began on 14 March, and from Hangoe alone some 11,000 Finns departed, taking with them only such goods as they could carry. Above is seen the dramatic moment when three Russian soldiers first face a Finnish sentry across the barbed wire on the new boundary.

MR. SUMNER WELLES'S EUROPEAN TOUR. On 25 February, Mr. Sumner Welles, U.S. Under-Secretary of State, and special envoy of President Roosevelt, arrived in Rome where he had the first of a series of exploratory talks on the European situation. Later he visited Berlin, Paris and London. The object of his visit was to gather first-hand information on the war situation for President Roosevelt, but he did not reveal the nature of the conversations he had with the heads of the various states. Above he is seen (left) with Viscount Halifax.

HITLER AND MUSSOLINI MEET. The meeting between the German and Italian dictators at Brennero on 18 March aroused world-wide speculation. It was reported from Rome that it was in connexion with a peace proposal of eleven points which Hitler had drawn up and shown to Mr. Sumner Welles. Mussolini, it was said, hoped to persuade the Fuehrer to modify them. In the light of later events, however, it seems much more probable that the meeting was to put the final touches to the agreement defining the part Italy was to play in the war.

AUSTRALIAN CRUISER AT SYDNEY. H.M.A.S. "Perth," cruiser of the Royal Australian Navy, to which she was presented by Britain, was welcomed on 31 March in Sydney Harbour, after she had steamed over 52,000 miles since the outbreak of the war. She is seen above passing through the Panama Canal on her way to Australian waters. Below, some of her officers and men, with fixed bayonets gleaming in the sunlight, march through the streets of Sydney while the Commonwealth crowds pay homage to their very own ship.

NEW ZEALANDERS IN TRAINING. New Zealanders to the number of 60,000 enlisted as volunteers in the Dominion's Expeditionary Force, apart from Air Force and Naval enrolments, before compulsory service was introduced early in 1940. The New Zealanders who came to Britain included a contingent of Maoris, some of whom are seen (top) giving their war cry. Below, New Zealand troops of an anti-tank unit are going on a " shingle-sledge " pulled by a light tractor to see what damage their fire has done to the moving targets.

British destroyer goes down fighting 8 April, 1940

H.M.S. "GLOWWORM" SUNK. On 8 April the British mine-laying destroyer, "Glowworm," whilst carrying out duties off Norway, ran into a strong enemy force of destroyers and light cruisers and was sunk after a gallant fight. These pictures, taken from a Nazi warship, show (top) the destroyer laying a smoke screen immediately before she went down, and (below) oil-covered survivors being picked up by a German ship.

NAZI TROOPS LAND IN COPENHAGEN. The war, which had languished strangely since October, 1939, suddenly took a dramatic turn when in the early hours of 9 April, Germany invaded Denmark and Norway. Here German troops are seen disembarking in Copenhagen from one of the many ships which ferried them across the Baltic. Meanwhile motorized units had invaded the country from the south. Denmark was unable to do more than protest at this flagrant violation of her territory. In a memorandum, Hitler attempted to justify his invasion by the absurd claim that Great Britain and France were about to invade Scandinavia themselves.

GERMAN INVASION OF NORWAY. The Nazi seizure of Oslo was a masterpiece of treachery. For months Germany had been scheming with a group of Norwegian traitors led by Major Quisling. The invasion was brilliantly planned and executed. All strategic points were occupied simultaneously. The Norwegians, ill-prepared for resistance, were dazed by the speed of the occupation and the paralysis of the machinery of government engineered by Quisling. The occupation of Oslo was typical. The forts in the fjord were given

bands paralyse Norwegian resistance

orders not to fire and the electrically controlled mines were disconnected. Air raid alarms sounded but German planes dropped leaflets, not bombs. The population was the more deceived by the arrival of military bands which played steadily for hours, watched by the astonished citizens. Meanwhile, tanks and guns had been poured into the city. The pictures show: (top left) Anti-aircraft gunner in the docks; (bottom left) tanks leaving the harbour; (top right) a German band playing; and (bottom right) Nazi troops receiving arms from lorries.

OCCUPATION OF NARVIK. Britain announced her intention on 6 April of mining Norwegian waters. This was used by Hitler as an excuse for his invasion of Norway. In fact his forces sailed before the British announcement and German destroyers entered Narvik Fjord on 9 April. They torpedoed two Norwegian warships and disembarked stores and troops (top). Next day five British destroyers, led by Captain Warburton-Lee in H.M.S. "Hardy," attempted recapture. They were driven back and Captain Warburton-Lee was killed, but they inflicted tremendous damage on enemy shipping as can be seen from the lower picture. Captain Warburton-Lee (inset) was posthumously awarded the Victoria Cross.   *(Lower photograph. British Official: Crown Copyright Reserved)*

Nazi troops land at Trondheim

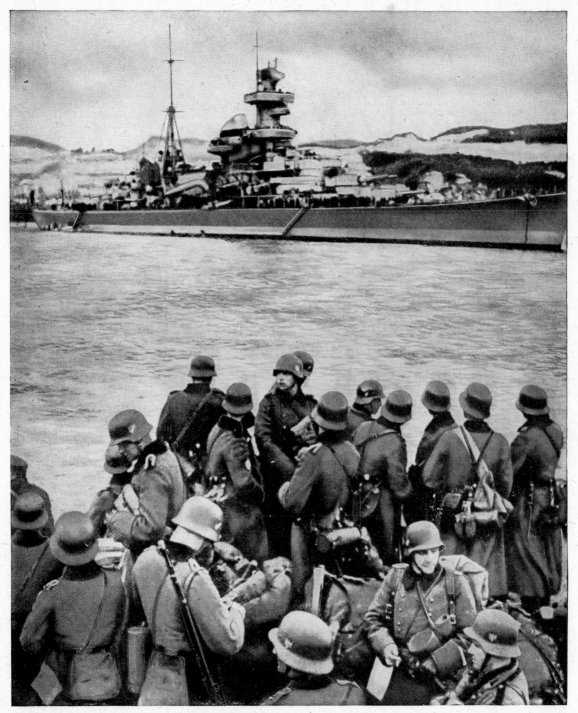

GERMAN CRUISER IN NORWEGIAN PORT. Hitler was prepared to pay any price for the speedy capture of Norway and flung the small German Navy recklessly into the attempt. It suffered fearful losses from British submarines, surface ships and aeroplanes, which sank between them several capital ships and destroyers, but it achieved its purpose of diverting the British Navy's attention from German troopships and transports which were rushing men and ammunition into Norway as fast as they were able. This picture, taken in Trondheim Harbour, shows Nazi troops being disembarked by tender from a German heavy cruiser of the "Hipper" class. The German capture of the port of Trondheim was to prove a decisive factor in the later struggle for Norway.

BOMBING OF ELVERUM. The little town of Elverum, at the mouth of the Oester Valley, and a vital junction on the railway from Oslo to Trondheim, suffered an hour's intensive bombing by Nazi warplanes on 9 April. Two days later, only an hour after King Haakon with the Norwegian Government had passed through in their flight from Oslo, it was bombed again and reduced to ruins. Above, the town hall is seen blazing furiously after being hit by incendiary bombs. The king eventually escaped by way of Neubergsund and Molde to Great Britain.

NAZI TANKS AND INFANTRY PRESS ON IN NORWAY. Having consolidated their positions in Southern Norway, German troops pushed rapidly inland in order to join up with the troops from Bergen, Trondheim and elsewhere. Norway's small army could do little—the capture of the chief ports had disorganized mobilization and robbed it of its arsenals. Nevertheless, it fought gallantly against the invaders. The pictures show: (top) German infantry taking up positions on a lakeside road; (below) tanks being ferried across a fjord on huge pontoons.

R.A.F. RAID STAVANGER AND BERGEN. The Nazi occupation of Norway was not long to go unchallenged, and when, on 11 April, Mr. Churchill promised that the Allies would aid Norway "to the best of their ability," R.A.F. bombers had already begun operations against the invader. From bases in Britain bomber squadrons launched a series of attacks on the German-occupied aerodrome at Stavanger, Norway's largest and most modern airfield. Their bombs wrought great damage both to the field and to enemy machines on the ground. The picture on the left, taken from one of the attacking planes, clearly shows a bomb bursting near two enemy

aerodromes and aircraft in Norway

machines. Another bomb has hit the end of the concrete runway. Several more machines in the picture have been severely damaged. Craters on the aerodrome show where other bombs have fallen. The picture on the right shows an attack on German seaplanes anchored off Bergen. The white cigar-shaped object at the top left of the picture is a bomb falling close to the lens of the camera. The Germans gained a decisive advantage by occupying all the aerodromes in Norway, thus preventing the Allies from using fighter planes, so necessary to counteract the almost ceaseless activity of the Nazi bombers. (*British Official Photographs: Crown Copyright Reserved*)

SECOND BRITISH ATTACK ON NARVIK FJORD. The British attack of 10 April on enemy warships and transports in Narvik Fjord had been beaten off. In the port there still remained several enemy destroyers. The Admiralty therefore decided upon a second attack, and on 13 April the 30,600-ton battleship "Warspite," flying the flag of Vice-Admiral Whitworth and accompanied by nine destroyers, steamed through the narrow entrance to the fjord. Contact with the enemy was made shortly before 12.30 p.m. and by 2 o'clock the battle developed into a series of running fights between the British ships and seven enemy destroyers. By 2.30 three of the enemy had been destroyed and shore batteries near Narvik had been silenced by "Warspite's" guns,

assisted by H.M.S. "Cossack," of "Altmark" fame, which went close in to the harbour and silenced an enemy howitzer. Meanwhile, four enemy destroyers fled up Rombaks Fjord, above Narvik, in an effort to escape. Right to the top of the nine mile stretch of water they were relentlessly pursued. When they could go no farther they were beached and abandoned by their crews. With seven enemy destroyers to their credit the Navy had done a good day's work and avenged the death of the heroic Captain Warburton-Lee, who had commanded the first attack (described on page 108). This reconstruction, by Frank Mason, R.I., shows H.M.S. "Warspite" with attendant destroyers in the thick of the battle. *(Reproduced by permission of the Northern Aluminium Company Ltd.)*

BRITISH TROOPS LAND IN NORWAY. The help which the British Government had promised to Norway was not long in forthcoming, and on 15 April it was announced that troops had made landings at several points and were establishing contact with the Norwegian forces. During the 400-mile voyage lifebelts were worn by the troops as seen in the picture below. Top picture shows a transport steaming into a Norwegian fjord. The landing was carried out without the loss of a single man. *(Lower photograph. British Official: Crown Copyright Reserved)*

GERMANS ATTACK BRITISH TRANSPORTS AND BOMB NORWEGIAN TOWNS. As one of the British transports was nearing its destination British destroyers detected the presence of an enemy submarine and attacked it with depth charges which forced it to the surface in a damaged condition. The top picture shows the U-boat after the attack; the black dots in the water are members of the crew swimming away from the damaged submarine. The bottom picture shows a German warplane bombing the little Norwegian town of Rena.

117

DIRECT HITS ON NAZI STORES IN NORWAY. On 25 April, the R.A.F. carried out an extensive series of raids on Nazi supply centres. The picture above shows large wharf warehouses ablaze during a raid on Hardanger Fjord, near Bergen, where the Germans had established a base for their troops fighting in Southern Norway. During the whole of the Norwegian campaign bombers of the R.A.F., operating from Britain, ceaselessly harried the Nazi communications with considerable success. *(British Official Photograph: Crown Copyright Reserved)*

50 | LILLEHAMMER

GERMANS PUSH ALLIES OUT OF LILLEHAMMER AND STEINKJER. British troops which had landed south of Trondheim linked up with the Norwegians fighting north of Oslo. Near Lillehammer they met powerful Nazi columns and, after fierce fighting, were forced to retire on 25 April. Farther north, British troops pushing south from Namsos occupied Steinkjer, but had to retire on 24 April owing to enemy bombing. The pictures show German troops advancing towards Lillehammer (top) and (below) Nazi infantry near Steinkjer.

BOMBING OF THE BRITISH BASE AT NAMSOS. Namsos, a pretty little Norwegian port situated at the head of the Namsen Fjord, north of Trondheim, was one of the places selected by the Allied High Command for landings in Norway. It became the main base for British forces operating against the Germans in the Trondheim area from the north, and from the moment the British arrived it was subjected to ceaseless bombardment from the air. At first the German airmen concentrated only on military stores and ammunition dumps, but soon the

whole town became a target, and its houses and churches were reduced to a shambles of blackened ruins and fallen masonry. It was here that Britain's lack of airfields in Norway was most keenly felt, for, being denied the use of fighter planes, there was nothing the troops could do to stave off the attacks, which in the end rendered the base untenable and forced the Allied forces to withdraw from Central Norway. This picture shows the utter desolation that resulted after the high explosive and incendiary bombs had done their deadly work.

GERMAN BOMBERS DESTROY BRITISH BASE. Aandalsnes, standing at the head of Romsdals Fjord, south of Trondheim, was another place chosen for Allied landings and, like Namsos, was the object of incessant bombing raids by the German Air Force from the moment the Allies arrived. It was from here, too, that the evacuation of Allied forces began on 2 May. The picture above, showing clouds of smoke rising from the flaming town, gives some idea of the terrible conditions under which the evacuation was carried out.

BOMB DAMAGE IN NARVIK. Although the southern parts of Norway had been evacuated, fighting continued in the north. The mountainous character of the country with its deep valleys and pine woods, and its ragged coastline made Norway difficult for the Nazis to over-run. In the north Narvik became the main focus of war. The pictures above show (top) German transports and supply ships sunk in Narvik Harbour and (below) some of the inhabitants driven from their homes by incendiary bombs which fell on many houses in the town.

123

Canadians mount guard at the Palace

DOMINION TROOPS GUARD THE KING. The Canadian forces, whose first contingents with their commander, Major-General McNaughton, had arrived in England in December, 1939, received a signal honour four months later when they were called upon to take over guard duties at the royal palaces. The first to mount guard were the Toronto Scottish, whose band (above) is seen marching across the parade ground at their British camp. Below, French Canadians of the First Division are marching up to Buckingham Palace to mount guard.

ANZACS HONOUR THEIR PREDECESSORS. On 25 April, Australian troops in the Near East celebrated the twenty-fifth anniversary of the landing at Gallipoli in 1915 by their fathers, the first Australians to make military history in the Northern Hemisphere. It was their deeds which did so much to win for Palestine and the Levant the liberty which their sons were now armed to defend. In Jerusalem, Australian troops (above) marched to attend a wreath-laying ceremony by Palestine's High Commissioner on the Australian memorial at Mount Scopus.

FIRST BOMB DEATHS IN ENGLAND. On 30 April, England suffered its first civilian casualties when a German mine-laying bomber was shot down and crashed into the garden of a house at Clacton, Essex. After tearing its way through several houses, it blew up. Two people in addition to the crew of the machine were killed, and 160 were injured. The town's A.R.P. services were called out and carried out their duties promptly and efficiently. The top photograph conveys some idea of the extent of the damage. The mass of twisted metal on the left is one of the engines of the machine, whilst on the right is seen all that was left of the aeroplane itself.

CANADIANS FIGHT WITH BRITAIN. In May, Canada's war effort had called up almost 100,000 men. Canadian troops fought side by side with British in Belgium and North France, a second division was almost in readiness for dispatch overseas, and a third in training in Canada. The Dominion's newly appointed Governor-General, the Earl of Athlone (above) is inspecting Canadian infantry in England on the eve of his departure for Canada; (below) Canadian troops in training with their field guns. *(Lower picture: Canadian Military Photograph)*

New Zealand troops in Western Desert

ANZACS ON GUARD IN EGYPT. The defence of Egypt and of British interests in the Eastern Mediterranean was the special task of troops from Australia, New Zealand and India, many of whom were stationed in the Western Desert, the 200,000-square-mile sand sea on the Egyptian-Libyan border, ready to deal instantly with any threat from Italy or elsewhere. Above, New Zealanders at a desert post freshen up their Bren gun technique; below, leaving their parade ground for a route march. (*British Official Photographs: Crown Copyright Reserved*)

BRITISH FLEET PLAYS ITS PART IN THE EVACUATION OF NORWAY. The successful evacuation of the Allied forces from Namsos and Aandalsnes early in May was in large measure due to the brilliant work of the Royal Navy. Approaching close to the coast, they put up a covering fire with their heavy guns and helped to keep the enemy in check whilst the troops were taken off. These pictures show an attack on a British aircraft carrier. Top right, a salvo of bombs is seen exploding just in front of an aircraft carrier. Bottom right, is a view from the deck of one of the following ships. Bottom left, is a photo of the explosions, taken from the deck of the aircraft carrier. Top left, anti-aircraft pom-poms going into action against the German planes.

ALLIED TROOPS LEAVE NAMSOS AND AANDALSNES. The enormous German air superiority in Norway made it impossible for the Allies to maintain, from the bases they had established, their forces in the field, and the Allied High Command was reluctantly obliged to withdraw its troops. The withdrawal was an extremely hazardous operation, but with the help of the Royal Navy it was carried out with a minimum of loss. The Allies lost three destroyers and one sloop, "Bittern." The top picture shows oil burning on the surface after the "Bittern" had sunk. Below, French troops are seen on board a British warship on their way to Britain.

INVASION OF THE LOW COUNTRIES

10 MAY, 1940. BLITZKRIEG BEGINS. Suddenly the terror so long awaited fell upon the Low Countries. German troops marched into Holland, Belgium, and Luxembourg. The enemy employed sinister and new forms of warfare against these unoffending peoples whose only crime was their neutrality: parachute troops, dropping from the sky on country roads and even city streets, created havoc everywhere; mechanized juggernauts, rumbling across the country, caused the civil population to flee in terror with such few possessions as they could carry, congesting the roads and impeding the attempts of the defending armies to hold the enemy. Typical scenes of the invasion are woven together to form this picture, specially drawn by Terence Cuneo.

NAZIS ATTACK HOLLAND FROM THE AIR. Shortly after 4 a.m. on Friday, 10 May, the peace of Holland's countryside was broken by the drone of aircraft and the skies were filled with white objects floating earthwards, the vanguard of Germany's army of paratroops. With machine guns, portable wireless transmitters and even folding bicycles, they descended on Holland and established themselves in fields, behind dykes and in empty houses. One detachment seized the aerodrome at Rotterdam, whilst others landed at Delft, four miles south of The Hague, and tried to cut off the Dutch capital. Throughout the day parachutists continued to land at strategic

by German paratroops

points all over Holland, and although they suffered severe casualties, many detachments succeeded in holding vital points and paving the way for further landings of men from troop-carrying planes. Numbers of paratroops are believed to have landed wearing Dutch uniforms, or disguised as civilians and even women. The pictures show (top left) paratroops being launched from a plane. Bottom left, their approach over the roof tops as they prepare to land in a Dutch village. In the picture above, a number of paratroops have just made a landing; the man in the background is " spilling " the air from his 'chute preparatory to unbuckling the harness.

R.A.F. RAID WAALHAVEN AERODROME, NEAR ROTTERDAM. Waalhaven was one of the first German objectives in Holland, and here the enemy consolidated their position. Dutch artillery and the R.A.F. launched a furious attack upon the airfield. For six hours waves of planes launched their bombs with deadly accuracy. Direct hits were scored on the hangars, and the ground defences were reduced to impotence. The damage rendered the airfield unusable for a considerable period after the attack. The picture shows demolished hangars and other damage to the airfield. *(British Official Photograph: Crown Copyright Reserved)*

Child victim of Nazi bomb

GERMAN RAID ON AMSTERDAM. In spite of his solemn and oft-repeated declaration that he would never wage war against innocent women and children, Hitler launched his warplanes against many open towns in France, Belgium and Holland on the first day of his offensive. Amsterdam was one of the places visited by Nazi bombers, and much damage was done to life and limb as well as to property in the centre and outskirts of the city. The picture above shows a grief-stricken Dutch father, himself badly wounded by bomb splinters, gazing mutely outside his house at the dead body of his little daughter.

LUXEMBOURG OVERRUN. The Grand Duchy of Luxembourg, sandwiched precariously between France, Belgium and Germany, was sacrificed on the altar of aggression when Germany struck west on 10 May. With only a nominal army of some 250 men to defend its integrity, that little state could do no more than raise an ineffectual protest. The picture shows German armed motor cyclists crossing into Luxembourg on their way to meet the French troops which had gone to the assistance of the Grand Duchy.

NAZIS ON BELGIAN SOIL. In addition to their thrusts into Holland and Luxembourg, the Germans crossed the Belgian frontier at four points at dawn on 10 May. By demolishing bridges and railway lines the Belgians managed to hold up the enemy advance on the first day, whilst German engineers worked furiously to repair the damage. The pictures show Nazi railway engineers hurrying along the line on repair trucks (top). Below, troops and equipment are being ferried across a river on rafts.

ALLIES GO TO BELGIUM'S AID. As soon as the news of Germany's violation of Dutch and Belgian neutrality became known the British and French Governments issued a joint announcement that immediate steps were being taken to aid the latest victims of Nazi aggression. Even before these words had been broadcast to the world, customs barriers were being raised and British and French mechanized columns were pouring across the frontier into Belgium. They were received with wild acclamation by the Belgian people who remembered how,

Belgium to stem German advance

twenty-six years before, aid had come from the same sources.   In the pictures we see: top left, a French tank passing a procession of farm carts loaded with child refugees; bottom left, Belgian townsfolk welcoming a British armoured car.   Top right, an Allied Bren gun detachment is watched by Belgian civilians as it passes through the main street of a frontier town.   Bottom right, Belgian soldiers fraternize with a lorry load of British soldiers who have come to fight beside them.   (*Photographs above and bottom left, British Official. Crown Copyright Reserved*)

BOMBERS DRIVE BELGIANS FROM THEIR HOMES. The stark tragedy of modern warfare is forcefully illustrated in these pictures of Belgian refugees fleeing before the advancing German armies. Taking with them as many personal belongings as they could carry, they thronged the roads in a pathetic trek to safety, harassed as they went by machine gun and bombing attacks from Nazi warplanes. The retreating refugees constituted a grave problem for the defending forces as the roads became so blocked with people and

before the Nazi terror

vehicles passing in the opposite direction that it was only with the greatest difficulty, and after much delay, that reinforcements and military traffic of all kinds could make their way to the front. The pictures show: top left, refugees leaving a shattered French town carrying their belongings; bottom left, an aged Belgian couple, fleeing before the invader, take a much needed rest by the roadside; above, refugees passing through a blazing village in their flight from the bombs. *(Top left and above photos, British Official; Crown Copyright Reserved)*

SIR ARCHIBALD SINCLAIR

**THE RT. HON.
WINSTON S. CHURCHILL**

MR. ERNEST BEVIN

MR. A. V. ALEXANDER

Previously Mr. Churchill had held Cabinet office as First Lord of the Admiralty; Mr. Attlee and Sir Archibald Sinclair were Leaders of the two Parliamentary Oppositions, Labour and Liberal respectively; Mr. Greenwood, Secretary of the Labour Party Research Department; Mr. Alexander, Leader of the Parliamentary Co-operative Party; Mr. Morrison, Leader of the London County Council; Mr. Bevin, member of the Executive of the Trades Union Congress, and Mr. Dalton, a member of the Labour Party's National Executive.

MR. HERBERT MORRISON

MR. C. R. ATTLEE

MR. ARTHUR GREENWOOD

MR. HUGH DALTON

RESIGNATION OF MR. CHAMBERLAIN. Confidence in the Government led by Mr. Chamberlain was seriously undermined by the general conduct of the war, and after a debate on the question in the Commons on 8 May, Mr. Chamberlain invited the Opposition to serve under him in a reconstructed Cabinet. Labour, however, refused and on 10 May the Premier resigned and was succeeded by Mr. Winston Churchill. Above is seen the new Premier together with some of the new Ministers. The new War Cabinet consisted of the Premier, who also became Minister of Defence; Mr. Chamberlain, Lord President of the Council; Lord Halifax, Foreign Secretary; Mr. C. R. Attlee, Lord Privy Seal, and Mr. Arthur Greenwood, Minister without Portfolio. Other Ministers were: Mr. A. V. Alexander, Admiralty; Mr. Anthony Eden, War; Sir Archibald Sinclair, Air; Sir John Simon, Lord Chancellor; Sir Kingsley Wood, Exchequer; Sir John Anderson, Home Secretary; Lord Lloyd, Colonies; Sir Andrew Duncan, Board of Trade; Mr. Herbert Morrison, Supply; Mr. Duff Cooper, Information; Mr. Ernest Bevin, Labour and National Service; Mr. L. S. Amery, India and Burma; Mr. Malcolm MacDonald, Health; Lord Woolton, Food; Viscount Caldicote, Dominions; Mr. Ernest Brown, Scotland; Lord Beaverbrook, Aircraft Production; Mr. H. Ramsbotham, Education; Mr. Robert Hudson, Agriculture; Sir John Reith, Transport; Mr. Ronald Cross, Shipping, and Mr. Hugh Dalton, Economic Warfare.

ANTI-ALLIES DEMONSTRATIONS IN ROME. Relations between the Allies and Italy had been strained before and since the outbreak of war, but it was not until May that the Italian Press seriously began a campaign of hate against the Allies. The Italian people as a whole had little or no dislike of the Western powers, but amongst the student class officially inspired demonstrations against the Allies broke out in many Italian cities. The picture shows Italian students in Rome giving vent to their dislike for the Allies.

GERMANS OVERRUN HOLLAND IN A FIVE-DAY CAMPAIGN. Whilst Nazi paratroops were landing behind the Dutch lines, armoured columns were crossing the frontier. By the night of 10 May these had advanced to the Maas, crossed the river, and entered Maastricht. The following day they crossed the Albert Canal over a bridge which, for some mysterious reason, had not been blown up by the defenders. Farther north the enemy crossed the River Yssel, near Arnhem, and by 12 May both the Maas and Yssel had been crossed at several points, and the Dutch troops were falling back. By 13 May the situation had become

so serious that Queen Wilhelmina and the Dutch Government sought refuge in England. Meanwhile German forces advancing in North Brabant had captured the Moerdyk Bridge which connects that province with South Holland, and armoured columns in the very heart of the country established contact with the air-borne troops that had been landed in the opening days of the campaign. Rotterdam fell, and at 1 a.m. on 14 May the Dutch commander gave up further resistance. The picture shows German troops paddling across the Maas at Maastricht in rubber boats, near the ruins of a bridge destroyed to impede their advance.

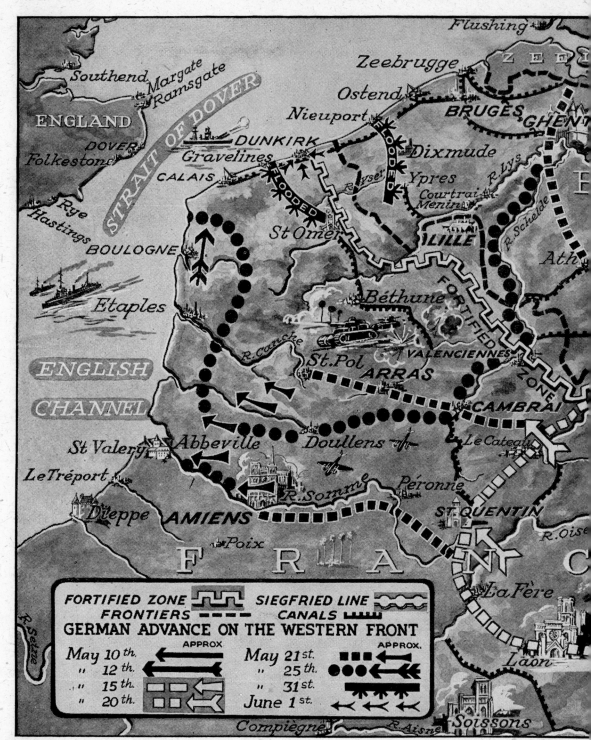

GERMAN ADVANCE FROM 10 MAY TO 1 JUNE. Germany's brilliant plan of campaign in Northern France and Belgium consisted of a wide sweep through the Low Countries, to draw the Allied armies northwards, followed by a swift thrust against the French right flank near Sedan, and an advance towards the coast to cut the Allied armies in two and encircle their left wing. The French were taken completely by surprise when the Germans on 14 May hurled their armoured divisions against the comparatively lightly held defences near

Sedan, and drove a rapidly enlarged bulge into the French lines. After Boulogne had fallen on 23 May the Germans violently attacked the Belgian left flank, and Belgium surrendered on 28 May, leaving the British front unsupported. The Allies fell back towards Dunkirk, whence they were evacuated by sea, and Belgium, Holland and all France north of the Somme were thus now in German hands. The arrows indicate the spearheads of the enemy attack; the lines show the positions reached by the German advanced troops on various dates.

R.A.F. ATTACK TRANSPORT COLUMN. Although the Royal Air Force was numerically inferior to the Luftwaffe, its pilots and its machines were far superior to those of the enemy. Throughout the campaign in Belgium and France, the R.A.F. continually harassed enemy communications, transport columns, railway sidings and marshalling yards, to retard the enemy advance. In the face of intense anti-aircraft fire and attacks from German fighter planes, the British bomber pilots flew low over their targets and released their bombs with deadly accuracy. This remarkable picture shows an attack on a German transport column passing through a small town. Bombs can be seen bursting close to the road and railway yards, while to the right another "stick" of bombs can be seen in the air. (*British Official Photograph: Crown Copyright Reserved*)

Nazi tanks and infantry sweep on

GERMANS PRESS HOME THE ATTACK IN BELGIUM. After crossing the Albert Canal on 11 May the Germans advanced towards Tongres and Waremme. Troops that had crossed the frontier farther north pushed southwards, their objective being the eastern end of the Liége-Louvain-Brussels railway. The Belgian Army which had taken up positions on the Meuse and the Albert Canal was forced to fall back on the second line of defence after making an heroic stand against the German mechanized units. British and French forces were rushing up in support. The top picture shows German soldiers making a dash across an exposed railway line. Below are German tanks advancing through a small town along the shallow bed of a canal—an easier mode of progress than the congested and damaged roads of Belgium.

BRUSSELS IN FLAMES AFTER AIR BOMBARDMENT. On 15 May the German High Command announced that it no longer regarded Brussels, historic capital of Belgium, as an open town. It stated that air reconnaissance had established beyond doubt that military columns were moving through the city, and that the German Air Force intended, therefore, to attack all military objectives. Even before this, and until the fall of the city on

17 May, Brussels was subjected to repeated and destructive German air attacks both with high explosive and incendiary bombs. The worst raid took place on Sunday, 12 May, when waves of German bombers destroyed many of the buildings on the outskirts of the city. The picture shows firemen dealing with the effects of a bomb which had exploded and wrecked shops and dwelling houses in one of the main streets of the city.

DRIVE TOWARDS THE FRANCO-BELGIAN FRONTIER. While the Belgian fortress at Liége still held out, the German attack south-west of the city pressed forward towards Brussels and the real and ultimate objective, Northern France. This attack was slowed down by the fierce resistance of the Belgian troops, and the perpetual harassing of the advancing German columns by the British Air Force. Where the Belgian troops were forced to fall back, they destroyed bridges and means of communication. The picture shows a German light tank checked by a river, the bridge across which has been blown up.

French launch tank offensive north of Sedan

FRENCH TANKS IN ACTION. The outstanding feature of the German campaign in Holland and Belgium was their use of mechanized units. Tanks and armoured cars, supported by aircraft, led the German attack in all cases. Hurriedly organized defences were of little avail against this new method of warfare, and the Allies strove to effect a counter blow with similar weapons. On 14 May the first clash between French and German mechanized units was reported, and a few days later a French tank offensive was launched in the Sedan-Rethel area. The top picture shows French tanks crashing through a wood. Below, a French tank is seen standing in a village street near Rethel. In the background can be seen a barrier specially constructed to stop the progress of enemy tanks; it conceals a German motorized column held up by the French.

THE AGONY OF ROTTERDAM. Holland's decision to lay down her arms on 14 May followed the appalling German air attack on that day on her second greatest city. For three hours Rotterdam, without anti-aircraft defences, was continuously and ruthlessly bombed. An area of two square miles in the heart of the city (the large white patch in centre of the aerial photograph on the right) was completely devastated, killing 30,000 people. As the bombing ceased, vast conflagrations followed, and hundreds of terrified

Rotterdam is ruthlessly bombed

women and children who had sought refuge in shelters were drowned by the flooding from burst water mains.   On the left the doomed city at peace is seen from the air: to the right of the main street, the Coolsingel, rises the tower of the Town Hall, with the Post Office in the foreground.   After the bombardment (right) the line of the street could hardly be traced; the Town Hall is a wreck, and the newly built Stock Exchange a heap of rubble.   Two hospitals were destroyed.   *(Right-hand picture, British Official: Crown Copyright Reserved)*

TIDES OF WAR SWEEP ON. The "bulge," that master-stroke of German strategy, resisting all the Allies' attempts to close it, or to cut the vanguard's communications with their bases, steadily widened and deepened, and the German advance swept like a flood into Northern France. Bombarding every obstacle, they thundered on, reducing towns, villages and farmhouses to flaming ruins. Reaching the Meuse from

Liége to Namur on 14 May, their colossal concentration of tanks and aircraft pressed southward and westward, until, after the Belgian surrender on 28 May, the tide had engulfed all Holland, Belgium and France north of the Somme. Above, German soldiers, their bayoneted rifles at the carry, advance cautiously over the scorching streets of a burning town, preparing to deal with any enemy snipers lurking among the ruins.

159

BRITISH DEFENDERS OF LOUVAIN. One obvious result of the first stages of the "bulge" was an added pressure on Louvain and Liége. The former was held by the B.E.F., who resisted stubbornly. The picture above shows an anti-tank gun emplaced at a strategic point amidst houses which have been shattered by

Louvain as refugees leave the city

bombardment. On 15 May the B.E.F. evacuated Louvain, which was subjected to terrific shell fire. The picture above is only one of hundreds of similar scenes as the exhausted refugees hurriedly left their homes taking with them just what they could snatch of their personal belongings. (*British Official Photographs: Crown Copyright Reserved*)

HOISTING THE INVADERS' FLAG. On 17 May Brussels capitulated after it had been blasted and scarred by terrific aerial attacks with high explosive and incendiary bombs (see pictures on pages 152 and 153). Here is seen the German standard being flown over the captured city. Thus, for the second time in a quarter of a century, an enemy flag flew triumphantly over the Belgian capital. The enemy remained the same—only the symbol of its oppression had altered its design from the eagle to the swastika.

Weygand takes over in France's darkest hour

WEYGAND REPLACES GAMELIN. At the height of the battle of the "bulge" the world was astounded by the news that General Gamelin, Commander-in-Chief of the French Forces, had been superseded by the seventy-three-year-old General Maxime Weygand, hitherto Allied Commander in the Near East. Above, is the man of whom Marshal Foch, whose chief of staff the new Generalissimo had been for nine years, including the darkest days of the German advance of 1918, had said: "When France is in danger, send for Weygand."

Charles Cundall

BATTLE OF FLANDERS. The "bulge" deepened and widened towards the west, as a million men and unnumbered machines fought out their death struggle. Allied reinforcements were rushed up, but by 18 May France, her back to the wall, had called Marshal Pétain to join M. Reynaud's Government. The thrust, towards Paris, changed its direction on the 19th, and drove north-west towards the Channel ports with

the object of encircling the British and Belgian troops and driving a wedge between the British Expeditionary Force and the French northern armies. This drawing, specially prepared for this book by Charles Cundall, A.R.A., gives a vivid impression of the fighting during those dark and critical days. German heavy tanks, supported by dive-bombing planes, are advancing across shell-blasted fields towards their objective.

165

ADVANCE OVER THE RIVERS. By 20 May the Germans were approaching Amiens, and farther east advance detachments had reached the Aisne. Fully equipped to deal with all obstacles that might hold up their progress, they crossed the river by pontoon bridges, like that seen above, which could be rapidly erected. The speed with which the enemy succeeded in crossing France's water defences was largely responsible for the spectacular advances achieved by the Germans during the early stages of the struggle.

GERMANS REACH THE CHANNEL. The 21st of May was a day of disaster for Allied hopes. The Germans, capturing Amiens, Arras and Abbeville, reached the sea despite the most desperate resistance. On that day, too, was announced the capture of General Giraud, Commander of the French Ninth Army, with his whole staff. Above, he is seen arriving, a prisoner, at a German airport. Below, B.E.F. troops are following up a bombing attack through a wood. (*Lower picture, British Official Photograph: Crown Copyright Reserved*)

GERMAN AIR WARFARE ON CIVILIANS. In their efforts to enlarge the "bulge," the Nazis heralded the onrush of their spearhead formations by ruthless bombing of open towns. Continuous waves of bombers blackened the skies, wreaking destruction on town and village. These attacks led to a complete disorganization of civil life, for it was impossible to prevent the people from taking to the roads in quest of safety and causing congestion which impeded military attempts to hold the invader. The pictures show: top left, an open town

in Northern France as the raiders left it, the wrecked shop façade in the foreground still with grim humour advertising funeral furnishings; bottom left, a main street in another town one end of which has been reduced to a heap of fallen masonry; top right, a ward in a French hospital from which the patients, unprotected even by the Red Cross, have been hurried off in search of such shelter as the bombers may have failed to find; bottom right, the altar steps of a village church covered with debris from the shattered superstructure.

BLITZKRIEG TACTICS IN NORTHERN FRANCE. For their rush into Northern France the Germans used vast numbers of monster tanks, in advance of which dive bombers cleared away many ground obstacles. Light armoured car and motor cycle units followed to prepare the ground for the infantry. The pictures above show (top) a mixed motorized column passing through a French town wh·ch has been heavily bombed from the air; bottom, German re·nforcements crossing into France past a French customs post.

French artillery replies to the German attack

FRANCE'S GUNS HIT BACK. The French did all they could to slow down the German advance. While their tanks sought to hold up the Nazi onrush, Allied planes ceaselessly battered the German communications, and the mobile French 75 mm. guns, using armour-piercing shells, accounted for many of the enemy armoured vehicles. The top picture shows camouflaged French guns pounding the unseen invaders; below, a heavy calibre gun, mounted on a caterpillar tractor, is directing its fire against an advancing tank column.

FIRST BOMBS ON ENGLAND. When, on 25 May, for the first time since 1918, German bombs fell on English towns in Yorkshire and Essex, the long-awaited air attack found Britain well prepared. Eight civilians only were injured, and material damage was slight. Above, the guns of an east coast anti-aircraft battery are displaying the deadly accuracy of their aim by the even spacing of their bursts of shell fire; below, residents of a Yorkshire town are clearing away the debris caused by the nearby explosion of a bomb.

BRITISH AT MENIN GATE. In the last days of May the B.E.F., still assisted by the Belgian armies, held in bulldog grip the plains of Western Flanders behind Dunkirk, while the bulge on their right flank widened and the onrushing German mechanized columns moved to surround them and cut them off from the sea. Some of the fiercest fighting took place at Ypres, round the Menin Gate (seen above), the memorial to the British troops who fell in Belgium's defence during the war of 1914-18   *(British Official Photograph: Crown Copyright Reserved)*

ALLIES CAPTURE NARVIK. Although the Allied forces had withdrawn from Central Norway, the attack on Narvik continued. By 25 May the Allies were twelve miles away, and the main German force, withdrawing to Bjornfjell, left only 250 men to defend the town, which on the 28th fell to a joint British-Norwegian force. Above, French troops are crossing a railway cutting near Narvik; at the village of Bjervik, seen below in flames, landed part of the Allied force which eventually captured the town.

KING LEOPOLD ORDERS " CEASE FIRE." The bitterest blow the Allied cause had yet suffered came on 28 May, when the Belgian King ordered his troops to cease fire, leaving the Allied left wing undefended. His order, repudiated by his Cabinet as unconstitutional, was obeyed by the bulk of his troops. Above, the King, with his War Minister, General Denys, is seen, just after his surrender; below, Belgian infantry, on the last day of their participation in the struggle, are running to take shelter from an air bombardment.

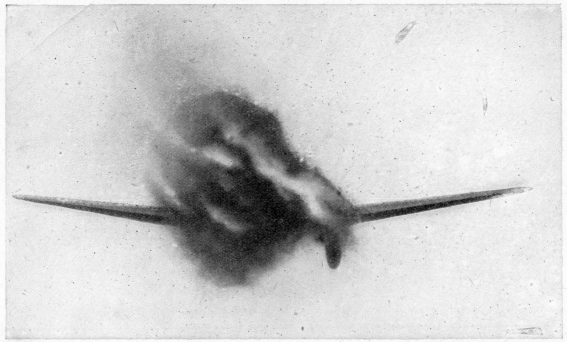

FAIREY "BATTLES" DO SOME "GROUND STRAFING." The R.A.F. made magnificent efforts to impede the Nazi attack on Northern France. By day and night ceaseless waves of "Wellington," "Hampden" and "Blenheim" bombers, eluding the enemy defences, went on to rain destruction on German communications behind the lines in the Rhineland and Holland, while over 1,500 enemy planes were brought down between the invasion of Belgium and the last week in May. One British squadron of twelve " Defiant " fighters shot down no less than thirty-seven enemy machines in a single day, 29 May, while other squadrons dropped water and

ammunition for the use of the garrison of British and French troops and marines who were heroically holding Calais against terrific German pressure during the Dunkirk evacuation. Meanwhile, as the Nazi troops moved, their mechanized columns and supply trains were riddled with machine gun fire from the air. Top left, a Heinkel, its engines and tanks ablaze, is about to crash in a heap of flaming wreckage. Bottom left, a low-flying plane secures a photo of the enemy horse transport column it is attacking. Right, Fairey " Battle " planes are ground strafing German motorized units with a salvo of incendiary bombs. (*British Official Photographs : Crown Copyright Reserved*)

177

Reproduced by permission of Northern Aluminium Co., Ltd.

EVACUATION OF THE B.E.F. FROM DUNKIRK

27 MAY—3 JUNE, 1940

"The most extensive and difficult combined operation in British naval history"—so the Admiralty communiqué of 3 June described the evacuation from Dunkirk. A fleet of 222 British naval vessels and 665 other craft took part in this drama of the sea, the latter manned largely by fishermen and yachtsmen, who, undismayed by enemy fire, as their boats were sunk or abandoned, transferred to other craft to continue the work of rescue. The flotilla included destroyers and tiny rowing boats, pleasure yachts and Thames tugs, Dutch motor vessels left in British ports after the invasion of Holland, and even a London Fire Brigade river-float, the "Massey Shaw," which, besides ferrying over 500 men from shore to the waiting transports, herself made the double crossing twice, each time with sixty men. The troops waded out to meet the tiny boats which carried them to the bigger craft used as transports, for the latter had to lie outside the shallows, half a mile from the shore. Of the naval vessels engaged, only six destroyers and twenty-four minor craft were lost, though throughout every moment of the operation incessant bombing attacks from the air, bombardment from land batteries on shore, and submarine and torpedo-boat attacks hampered the rescuers. Meanwhile British naval forces shelled enemy artillery positions on shore to protect the flanks of the withdrawing troops, and the R.A.F. battled with enemy planes above the crowded waters. This marvellous feat of skill and bravery, crowned, in the King's words, "by a success greater than we had ever dared to hope," will live for ever in the annals of all three arms of the British fighting forces. This picture, by Charles Cundall, A.R.A., depicts the scene off Dunkirk, as the rescued troops are rowed out to the waiting transports, under intense land and air bombardment, in tiny pleasure boats hitherto acquainted only with the pleasant waters of British south coast holiday resorts.

MARCH TO DUNKIRK. The laying down of their arms by the Belgian troops left the B.E.F. in Belgium and N.W. France in imminent danger of being surrounded and driven into the sea, for on 23 and 24 May the Germans had reached the Channel at Boulogne and Calais. German official communiqués confidently boasted of the inevitable annihilation of the whole British Expeditionary Force. An attempt to break through to the south to

join the French being hopeless, it was decided to fight a rearguard action and attempt withdrawal by sea. Harassed on every side and from the skies by the enemy, the wearied but dauntless British soldiers, many of them after a continuous fighting march from the Luxembourg border, fell back towards Dunkirk. Above, a few of them are seen marching into the town, which shows plentiful signs of the heavy bombardment to which it was subjected.

ON DUNKIRK BEACH. On 30 May the world heard that one of the most amazing military operations of all time was in progress. Many of the British troops had reached Dunkirk and were already being evacuated under the merciless fire of hundreds of German bombers, by a flotilla of 887 craft of every size and shape. The first men arrived in England on 30 May, the last on 3 June, over 330,000 in all reaching safety. In the upper picture, taken from a destroyer, troops are seen on the sands at Bray Dunes wading out waist-deep to meet the little

boats, two of which can be seen in the foreground, that will convey them to the rescuing ships. Below, troops are drawn up on a beach awaiting the strange navy gathering to take them to safety. During the entire time of their long wait for rescue, the men were subjected to almost continuous bomb and machine gun attack from German planes, which might have been considerably more serious than they were had it not been for British fighters and anti-aircraft batteries which engaged the raiders on the outskirts of the town.

183

SHIPS LEAVE DUNKIRK. Among the evacuees from Dunkirk were a number of wounded, both British and French, from the armies that had fought in the Battle of Flanders. These were, as far as possible, convoyed in ships painted white and marked with a Red Cross, but this did not relieve them from the attentions of the Nazi bombers. Above, a hospital ship is taking off wounded from a narrow jetty; below, a destroyer setting out with crowded decks for the voyage home to safety.

TROOPS WAIT FOR RESCUE. Waiting their turn to find places in the rescue vessels, the troops at Dunkirk scattered over the neighbouring sand dunes, taking such rough cover as they could find from the Nazi planes, and going down to the beach in batches as boats became available. This chain of men, neck-deep in water, but many still with their rifles and equipment, is wading out from the shore to scramble up the ship's side, hailed by their mates' cries from the deck: "Keep your socks dry."

REARGUARD COVERS THE DUNKIRK EMBARKATION. During the evacuation from the sands, thousands of men carried on a rearguard action on the outskirts of Dunkirk in order to hold up the advance of the enemy and draw off as far as possible the artillery attacks on the town and the rescue ships. Meanwhile, a small British detachment sent to hold Calais, to reduce German pressure on Dunkirk, held out against enormous odds for several days, thus contributing invaluably to the withdrawal of the main body of the British Expeditionary Force.

Practically the whole of this gallant little force was either killed or taken prisoner. To the last moment, unprotected even by dug-outs on the open ground, small groups of men armed only with ordinary service rifles did what they could to reply to the incessant bombing and machine gunning of the Nazi planes. Above one such defender is seen falling to a shrapnel hit, his rifle still defying the enemy in the skies. In the distance bombs aimed at the rescue ships raise huge columns of water as they fall quite harmlessly into the sea.

COVERING THE EVACUATION. The success of the Dunkirk operation was largely due to the work of the R.A.F., who, in Mr. Churchill's words, " decisively defeated the main strength of the German Air Force and inflicted a loss of nearly four to one." The ships were guarded on their Channel passage by Lockheed " Hudson " Coastal Command planes, one of which is seen above approaching Dunkirk. In the background smoke is rising from oil tanks destroyed by the R.A.F.   *British Official Photograph: Crown Copyright Reserved)*

DUNKIRK COMMANDERS LEAVE. Largely responsible for the success of the evacuation was Admiral Jean Abrial (above), Commander-in-Chief of the French naval forces at Dunkirk, who was among the last to leave the town, which was occupied by the Germans on 4 June. Not until four-fifths of his army was in safety did Lord Gort, British Commander-in-Chief, cross to England. Below, he is being welcomed by a commissionaire outside the War Office, an old comrade-in-arms of the war of 1914-18.

DUNKIRK MEN COME HOME. The ships which brought the Dunkirk heroes to safety were constantly attacked by Junkers dive bombers which flew low over them and strafed the crowded decks, but the guns of their naval escorts and the counter-attacks of the R.A.F. fighter planes were so effective that little damage befell them while crossing the open sea. Above is a view of two of the destroyers which acted as transports on their arrival at a home port. (*British Official Photograph : Crown Copyright Reserved*)

Dunkirk men welcomed home

TIRED BUT STILL CHEERFUL. The last men were withdrawn from Dunkirk on the night of 3-4 June, leaving the town unusable by the enemy. It had been thought at the beginning of the operation that twenty or thirty thousand men might be got away, but, though losses were considerable, the total number of Allied troops brought to safety reached the amazing figure of 335,000. Above, some of them are being welcomed with refreshments at a wayside station in England, tired out but still cheerful.

Little ships that did great work at Dunkirk   27 May–3 June, 1940

DUNKIRK ARMADA RETURNS. Many of the little boats used in the Dunkirk operation were manned by amateur crews, and came from the Thames and the coast towns of S.E. England. A Thames boat firm, acting as a clearing-house, collected small craft of all kinds, especially motor boats, from London's river. Many were damaged or sunk during the operations, but most returned, like those seen above as they are being towed up the Thames back to their "peace stations," to resume a calmer life as pleasure boats.

Navy blocks Zeebrugge as troops leave Dunkirk

NEW EXPLOIT AT ZEEBRUGGE. On 3 June the British Navy repeated an exploit of 1918 by sinking two cement-laden blockships (seen above) across the lock entrance to the canal at Zeebrugge, and destroying the sea gates and lock mechanism of the canal. No damage or casualties were suffered during the operation, which was carried out under heavy enemy machine gun fire and bombing from the air. Below, some wounded French soldiers, evacuated with the B.E.F. from Dunkirk, practise "thumbs up" on arrival at an English hospital.

PARIS BOMBED FROM THE AIR. The German sweep through France to the south was heralded on 3 June by a severe midday air raid on Paris. About 300 planes, twenty-five of which were shot down, flying at a height of five miles, dropped indiscriminately over 1,000 bombs, securing fifteen direct hits on a hospital, killing or wounding thirty children in one of the five schools hit, and inflicting many casualties, including over 250 deaths. The picture shows firemen and air raid wardens searching for victims in the ruins of a private house.

DRIVE TOWARDS THE FRENCH CAPITAL. On 5 June began the furious German onslaught on the Weygand Line. A heavy artillery and tank attack, followed up by half a million infantry covered by dive bombers, was thrust from the regions of Amiens and Laôn towards Compiègne. French anti-tank defences, hurriedly improvised, though supported by tank and air counter-attacks, could do little or nothing to stem the onset. The picture above shows German infantry leaving cover to follow up the advance of their mechanized units.

R.A.F. OVER GERMANY. Besides maintaining unceasing air attacks on the communications of the advancing Nazis in France, during the first days of June, R.A.F. bombers nightly raided oil depots, factories, and other military objectives in the industrial centres of North Germany, and many Ruhr and Rhineland towns; over 400 bombs were dropped in one raid on a Frankfurt oil depot on 4 June. Though German fighters and anti-aircraft guns, such as those of the coastal battery above, took their toll of victims, the defence proved **very ineffective** before the skill and resourcefulness of British pilots, nearly all of whom returned safely.

Germans sweep on towards Paris

THE ENCIRCLEMENT OF PARIS. On 7 June fresh masses of German troops attacked along the Somme and the Aisne, advanced units reaching Rouen on the 9th. The French were forced back on the Seine, which Nazi advance guards began to cross on 10 June, and the evacuation of Paris began as the Nazis moved to surround it from east, west and north. The pictures show two aspects of the German advance; top, Nazi infantry advance cautiously through an evacuated village; the man on the right has just been hit by a bullet from a sniper hiding in a ruined house. Bottom, German guns drawn up along a road are bombarding the French lines.

ITALY TAKES UP ARMS. Italian "non-belligerency" ceased on 10 June, when Mussolini threw off the mask, and in a speech from the balcony of the Palazzo Venezia, in Rome, announced war on Britain and France. America and other neutrals hailed the Duce's choice of the blackest hour in France's struggle as a "stab in the back." Italy made no immediate spectacular military move, confining herself at first to air warfare on Alexandria, Malta, Gibraltar, and other British naval stations and possessions within reach, and

submarine raids on British ships in the Mediterranean. To these the R.A.F. replied by an intensive air campaign against military objectives in Northern Italy, especially her great engineering centre, Turin, and on Libya, showing great superiority to the vaunted Italian Air Force, and wreaking enormous damage at comparatively little cost in pilots or machines. Left, Italian troops marching down the Passo Romano, Rome; above, Mussolini in company with his staff officers watches Italian planes take off on their first bombing raid on French territory.

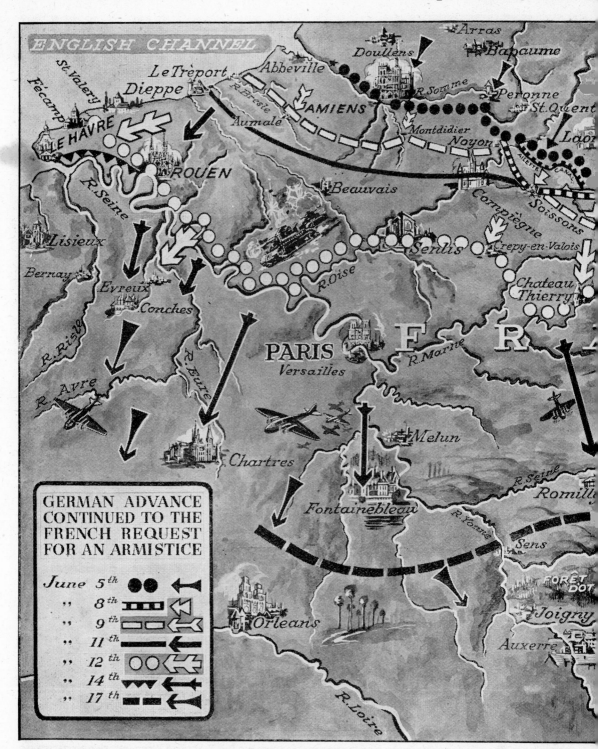

GERMAN ADVANCE FROM 5 JUNE TO 17 JUNE. A slight relaxation of enemy pressure in the first days of June was followed on the 5th by an advance over the Ailette Canal; on the 9th the Germans occupied Soissons. On 11 June the battle for Paris was at its peak, the enemy had reached the Seine and were attempting the crossing under smoke screens, while further east a salient was formed near Chateau-Thierry in an attempt to encircle

the capital. On the 14th Paris fell, the Allies falling back in an attempt to reform their line to the south. On the 15th the Seine was crossed east of Paris near Romilly, and German advance guards reached Chaumont, pressed on towards Dijon, and entered Verdun on the same day. On the 16th France asked for an armistice. The German advance continued until it was signed on the 22nd. The arrows show the direction of the main enemy thrusts.

W.I.P.—G*

GERMANS ENTER PARIS. On 11 June the French Government left Paris for Bordeaux, and on the 13th the military governor, General Hering, declared the capital an open town. War factories were blown up, and such machinery as could be dismantled sent south. The next morning the Germans entered the city,

the infantry preceded by motor cyclist and machine gun troops. Throughout the day the endless co'umns of Nazis goose-stepped through the deserted streets guarded by the disarmed police. The picture above, specially drawn for this book by Harold Forster, shows tanks and armoured cars passing the Arc de Triomphe.

PARIS IN NAZI OCCUPATION. As the Germans took over Paris from the French civil officials, the swastika flag was unfurled on the city's principal buildings, among them the Eiffel Tower, the Hôtel de Ville, the Hôtel Crillon, where the German staff established its headquarters, and, bitterest of all, the Arc de Triomphe, beneath which lies the tomb of France's unknown soldier of 1918. The pictures show: left, a Nazi heavy motorized unit, trailing a gun, passing the sandbagged obelisk, France's "Cleopatra's Needle," in the Place de la Concorde; above, German officers, accompanied by a French civil official, looking out over Paris from the top of the Arc de Triomphe, the swastika flag flying before them; below, crowds watching a German animal transport column passing a saluting base in the neighbourhood of the Arc de Triomphe.

MORE BRITISH TROOPS TO FRANCE'S AID. When the German onslaught on Paris was at its height, Mr. Churchill promised that all possible help would be sent to support France. On 15 June a reconstructed B.E.F. was ready to sail, among it men who but a fortnight before had escaped from Dunkirk. But with the collapse of France many a transport, like that seen above departing from an English port, its deck crowded with Canadians, was recalled when only a few miles from British shores. (*Canadian Military Photograph*)

AMERICANS IN BRITAIN GO HOME. Events in the Low Countries and France, and the expected blitzkrieg on Britain, caused the American Government to urge its nationals to leave the island at once. On 15 June the U.S. liner " Washington " (above, with passengers boarding from a tender) sailed from Galway with about 2,000 U.S. citizens. On its voyage the ship was stopped by a German submarine and the passengers were ordered to the boats, but after identification was allowed to proceed unharmed.

FRANCE GIVES UP. Paris had fallen, and the collapse of France followed. The Premier on the 16th resigned in favour of Marshal Pétain, who immediately asked Germany for an armistice, neglecting Churchill's offer of a Franco-British union of nations. Meanwhile German troops (top) advanced relentlessly south of Paris, reaching the Langres plateau on the 16th, and on the 18th occupying Belfort and Dijon. On the same day the fortress of Metz fell to the enemy. Below, Hitler is seen inspecting a French heavy tank destroyed by German fire.

HITLER AND MUSSOLINI MEET IN MUNICH. Using the Spanish dictator, General Franco, as mediator, Germany consented to France's request that negotiations should take place for ceasing hostilities, and, in Marshal Pétain's words, "concluding an honourable peace." Above, Mussolini and Hitler are seen driving through the streets of Munich on the 17th to their meeting for the settlement of the armistice terms; below, they are cheered by children after their conference. On the 18th the terms were sent to the French Government at Bordeaux. On the following day France named her plenipotentiaries for a conference at Compiègne where, twenty-two years before, Marshal Foch had met the German plenipotentiaries on a similar errand.

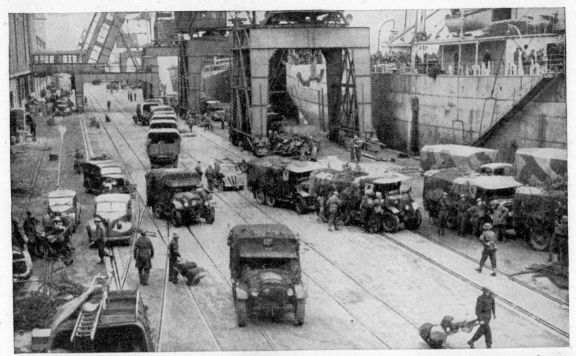

TOMMIES LEAVE FRANCE AGAIN.   The German drive to the west, and France's collapse, made it necessary to bring back the British troops who had been fighting in N.W. France before they could be surrounded. Brought up in camouflaged lorries (above) to Cherbourg and other ports, they marched along the quaysides (below) to cross the Channel, like the men of Dunkirk, in vessels of every kind, from liners to pleasure craft and tiny steam trawlers.   They landed at a port in Western England.   (*British Official Photographs : Crown Copyright Reserved*)

HITLER AND MUSSOLINI GLOAT OVER FRANCE. The dictators celebrated the fall of France with triumphal rejoicing. Hitler ordered flags to be flown throughout the Reich for ten days, and church bells to be rung daily for a week. In Paris, German troops with cameras and guide books wandered about sight-seeing. Above, with Goering, followed by German staff officers, Hitler is viewing a captured portion of the Maginot Line; below, Mussolini stands in a camouflaged car, touring the battlefront in South-East France.

STAGE SET FOR FRANCE'S HUMILIATION. By Hitler's express orders the stage set for the signing of the Franco-German armistice was exactly the same as on November 11, 1918, when Foch met the German plenipotentiaries on a similar errand. Then the armistice had been signed in a railway coach in the forest of Compiègne. Since 1918 that historic coach had been kept in the Invalides in Paris whence it had been moved after the Treaty of Versailles. Hitler ordered it to be taken to the exact spot in the forest where the act that marked the cessation of hostilities in 1918 had taken place. On that occasion France was the victorious dictator of terms. Hitler could not have conceived a plan more hurtful to the French pride than this resetting

of the scene of her earlier triumph. These scenes of the historic meeting show, top right, the coach being moved up into the exact position it occupied in 1918; top left, a German guard of honour marches round it and the memorial to Germany's 1918 defeat, seen in the left of the picture; bottom left, the French delegates (left to right): General Huntziger, Admiral Le Luc and General Bergeret, followed by M. Léon Noël, in civilian dress, and accompanied by German officials, arrive for the ceremony of the signature; bottom right, Hitler, with General von Brauchitsch and Admiral Raeder on his right and Goering on his left, followed by Ribbentrop and Hess, leaving the scene after the signature. Afterwards the historic coach was removed to Berlin.

FRANCO-GERMAN ARMISTICE SIGNED. At 2.45 p.m. on 21 June, Hitler entered the famous railway carriage at Rethondes, in the Forest of Compiègne, occupying Foch's chair. A guard of German infantry and airmen was drawn up outside the carriage. General Keitel read Hitler's message and the armistice terms to the French delegates; Hitler left after the preamble had been read. The historic scene and its

setting, specially drawn by T. C. Dugdale, A.R.A., is shown above; the Germans (left to right) are Admiral Raeder, Goering, Hitler, General Keitel, General von Brauchitsch, Hess; the French, General Bergeret, M. Noël, General Huntziger, Admiral Le Luc. In the foreground is Ribbentrop. The armistice was signed by the French on the following day in the same surroundings; afterwards the coach was taken to Berlin.

PART OCCUPIED BY GERMANY

PART DEMILITARISED BY FRANCE

Naval Bases thus:- **BREST**

GERMANY OCCUPIES HALF FRANCE. The map shows the full extent of French humiliation under the very severe terms of Germany's armistice. All North and West France (tinted grey above), her richest provinces, including Paris itself and the whole Channel and Atlantic coastline with its naval bases, were to be occupied at French cost by Germany till the end of the war, while a wide strip (black) along her Italian frontier was demilitarized; all French forces in these areas were to lay down their arms before removal to the unoccupied area for demobilization; French administration might be carried on from any selected town in unoccupied France, or, by arrangement with Germany, from Paris; for the time being the French chose Vichy.

FRENCH SOLDIERS CROSS THE BORDER. During the armistice negotiations the remorseless enemy advance went on. On 17 June the Germans announced that the French in Alsace and Lorraine had been surrounded; on the 19th Toul and Lunéville were taken. On 20 June France's third largest city, Lyons, was occupied. As the Germans approached the Swiss frontier, some 50,000 French and Polish soldiers crossed into neutral territory; (above) a Swiss officer watches men crossing the border in a village partly Swiss, partly French, where presently Swiss soldiers (below) will pile the arms taken from them as they march off for internment.

BRITISH NAVY FIRES ST. MALO, BREST AND CHERBOURG. The last men of the second B.E.F., together with many French troops who were anxious to carry on the fight, embarked from Brest and Cherbourg only a few hours before these ports fell to the Germans. As at Dunkirk, the crossing to Britain was made in hastily collected vessels of every size and kind. Not only did the authorities manage to get away all the men of the second B.E.F., but also their full equipment and much of their base stores. Before leaving, the British

Allied troops leave for Britain

destroyed everything in the ports that could be of value to the enemy. British naval detachments aided by Royal Engineers demolished the harbour works at Brest, Cherbourg and St. Malo, rendering them useless. At St. Malo great fires (left) rose from petrol and powder stores as the last ship sailed; French troops (top right) leaving Brest Harbour, are watching warehouses go up in smoke, while after the demolition parties had done their work huge fires (bottom right) blazed everywhere among the debris of shattered harbour buildings.

BRITISH SUPREMACY IN MEDITERRANEAN. Italy's efforts to establish naval supremacy in Near Eastern waters were not marked by very conspicuous success. The capture of a submarine by any surface vessel is an almost unheard-of event in naval warfare; but on 22 June it was announced that the large Italian submarine "Galileo Galilei," captured by the British trawler "Moonstone," had been brought into harbour as a prize. On sighting the enemy's periscope "Moonstone" brought her to the surface with depth charges and replied

to her fire with her four-inch gun, four shells from which were enough to induce her to surrender. Above, "Moonstone's" prize is being towed into Aden Harbour. Below are two other aspects of war in the Mediterranean: right, Italian planes dropping salvoes of bombs at a British warship in what Italy prematurely called "our sea" demonstrate their bad marksmanship; left, another British warship, unable to find Il Duce's bashful navy, finds time to enjoy a little quiet gunnery practice. *(Top photograph, British Official: Crown Copyright Reserved)*

FRANCE ACCEPTS ITALIAN TERMS. At the Villa Inchesa, near Rome, on 24 June, France received Italy's armistice terms. Signed at 6.15 p.m. that day, they came into force, simultaneously with those of the Franco-German armistice, at 12.35 a.m. on 25 June, while Italian troops were still advancing on the Alpine front and had just occupied Mentone. They included demilitarization of zones in France, Tunis, Algeria and Somaliland; full rights for Italy over Jibuti and its railway; demilitarization of the French fleet, and the naval bases at Toulon, Oran, Bizerta and Ajaccio; control of all French airports, and the right to demand the surrender of all or part of the French arms which had been facing Italian forces. All Italian prisoners of war and internees

in French hands were to be handed over to Italy; free transport of goods was to be permitted between Italy and Germany through unoccupied French territory. Italy might demand that French ships should be used for minesweeping, but declared that she did not intend to use units of the French fleet for her own purposes during the war or to lay claim to it on the conclusion of peace. The Italian delegates were Marshal Badoglio (standing), Count Ciano (to his left), Admiral Cavagnari, Generals Pricolo and Roatta, representing the Italian Navy, Air Force and Army; the French were represented by (left to right above) Vice-Admiral Le Luc, M. Léon Noël, and Generals Huntziger, Parisot and Bergeret, the last named on behalf of the Air Force.

AUSTRALIAN TROOPS DISEMBARK. Towards the end of June the first considerable contingents of troops from Australia and New Zealand landed in Great Britain to prepare for active service by a period of intensive training in the Homeland. They came by way of Capetown in liners, escorted by a powerful convoy of ships of the British, Australian, New Zealand and Canadian Navies, which secured for them a completely uneventful voyage. Commanded respectively by Major-General Wynter, who served with the Anzacs of

1914-18, and Major-General Freyberg, V.C., hero of the Gallipoli landings of 1915, these magnificent troops of perfect physique and morale, including a battalion of Maoris and a detachment of the New Zealand R.N.V.R., were welcomed by a message from the King. The pictures show: left, Australians listening to their band on the quay immediately after disembarking at a Scottish port; right, more "Diggers" on a few days' leave in London, arriving at their temporary social headquarters, at the Strand Theatre, Aldwych, for pay-day parade.

THE ANZACS IN THE MOTHER COUNTRY. The troops from Australia and New Zealand came to Britain prepared to enjoy themselves and to make the most of their stay in the Homeland. They were determined also to show their taste for business as well as for pleasure. "I pity your enemies," said Mr. Geoffrey Shakespeare, Under-Secretary for the Dominions, welcoming them on their landing, "and I congratulate those fortunate enough to fight by your side." Top left, a contingent of Australians setting out from their

training camp, headed by their band and drum major, for a route march through the English countryside; bottom left, the King, on a visit to an Australian camp in Southern England, watches "Diggers" building gun emplacements with sandbags as they settle down in their new quarters. Top right, Queen Elizabeth, surrounded by officers and men of the navies, armies and air forces of all the Dominions, at the Victoria League Club in London: bottom right, Australians in happy mood marching through London streets on leave.

THE WATCH IN THE DESERT. The Italian declaration of war had been long expected, and from the beginning of the war full measures had been taken by Britain to protect Egypt and the Suez Canal against Italian attacks. Egypt did not herself undertake hostile action, though she stood ready to defend her territory, warning Italy that any attempt on Cairo would involve her entry into the war by Britain's side. The Red Sea coasts and the desert were ceaselessly guarded by British troops aided by New Zealand, Indian and Maltese contingents;

and the Nile was continuously patrolled by armed motor launches. The pictures show: top left, Arab soldiers holding look-out posts to guard against surprise landings by troops from Italy's African possessions on the Red Sea coast; bottom left, Egyptian soldiers in a sandbagged post guarding a bridgehead in Cairo; top right, men of an English county regiment at Bren gun practice over the sands; bottom right, British tanks and their crews in Cairo awaiting orders to move off into the desert. *(British Official Photographs: Crown Copyright Reserved)*

TARGETS OF THE NAZI BOMBERS. After the capitulation of France the German Air Force, no longer confining itself to coastal operations, greatly intensified its attacks on Britain, and from 18 June onwards numbers of enemy planes crossed the coast almost nightly. But the people of Britain were completely unmoved by these attacks. Material damage and casualties were surprisingly small, and R.A.F. fighters and anti-aircraft guns disposed of a heavy percentage of the attackers. In the first week of regular raiding at least

air raids on Britain

twelve machines were shot down, and a number more accounted for by anti-aircraft guns—an earnest of the amazing response that would be made to bigger attempts to come. The south coast village church (left), set on fire by incendiary bombs, in one of the first raids of the series is receiving attention from the local A.F.S.; right, an inn somewhere in Eastern England carries on in the open air after the interior had been wrecked, for it takes more than a Nazi high explosive bomb to rob a Briton of his glass of beer and game of darts !

WORK OF THE BOMBERS AND THEIR DESTRUCTION. Many of the bombs dropped by Marshal Goering's air force fell on residential areas and caused destruction and misery in the homes of peaceful working-class districts. What is left of a row of villas is seen in the lower picture on the left, while above,

dearly for their daring

one of the victims is removing some of his personal belongings from his Anderson shelter which has stood up to the impact of a nearby bomb. The heavy toll paid by the German raiders is illustrated by the bombers which have been brought down in the sea (top right), and in a garden in Southern England (bottom right).

AIR RAID DEFENCES IN ACTION. Britain's defences against the raiders proved themselves again and again. Bombers were repeatedly engaged by fighter aircraft and shot down, or were destroyed in the anti-aircraft barrage. Fighter pilots, constantly on the alert for raiders, are seen running to their machines

on receipt of an alarm (top left). Searchlights (bottom left) pick out the raiders and hold them in their beams whilst the A.A. guns (bottom right) or fighter pilots engage them. The balloon barrage (top right) which effectively prevents dive bombers from approaching their targets, has already several raiders to its credit.

CIVILIAN DEFENDERS OF BRITAIN.　The magnificent work of Britain's gallant airmen and anti-aircraft gunners was matched by the unfailing devotion to duty of all branches of the civil defence services.　Air raid wardens, firemen, ambulance drivers, stretcher and demolition parties, and all the other A.R.P. personnel were on duty day and night ready to assist in the defeat of the raiders.　The Volunteer Observer Corps (top left), who had watched and listened unremittingly since the beginning of the war, rendered valuable

service in detecting the approach of enemy aircraft. The Auxiliary Fire Service (a section of which is seen at practice in the picture, bottom left) proved itself time and time again to be perfectly capable of dealing with any fires caused by high explosive or incendiary bombs. Many of the large industrial firms trained and equipped their own A.R.P. squad. Above, a stretcher party in anti-gas clothing and respirators is seen removing a " casualty " during practice at a Lancashire pithead. They have since proved their merit to the full.

FREE FRENCHMEN RALLY TO THE FLAG. Under the inspired leadership of General de Gaulle, who is seen on the left, a rapidly growing army of free Frenchmen was enrolled in England to fight side by side with the British Army against the common enemy. Admiral Muselier (right), who made a thrilling escape from France in a destroyer, was appointed Commander-in-Chief of the Free French Navy. A number of vessels manned entirely by French officers and men took part immediately in successful operations.

Poles join their British Allies

POLISH TROOPS TO FIGHT WITH BRITAIN. The army of Free Frenchmen was not the only ally saved from the war in France. As soon as it became evident that France had decided to seek an armistice, large numbers of Polish soldiers were quickly transferred to England. They are here seen disembarking from a transport, resolved to prove, in the words of M. Jan Mikolajczyk, Vice-President of the National Council of the Polish Republic, "the will and determination to persevere in this struggle for the liberation of Poland."

REFUGEES ARRIVE AS PRISONERS LEAVE. The decision to demilitarize the Channel Islands produced many poignant scenes such as that pictured above, as whole families with what luggage they could carry sought safety in England. At the same time German prisoners of war, who are seen below marching to their embarkation station, were being sent for greater security to internment camps set up in Canada.

" ARANDORA STAR " SUNK BY U-BOAT. On 3 July news was received that the " Arandora Star," carrying 1,500 German and Italian internees to Canada, had been torpedoed and sunk by a German submarine. Many lost their lives through panic, in spite of the heroism of the British guards. Above, the liner is seen at the start of a peace time voyage ; below, are some of the survivors being landed at a Scottish port.

FRENCH WARSHIPS UNDER BRITISH CONTROL. When France laid down arms, Britain asked the Pétain Government to allow the French fleet, lest it fall into German hands, to sail for British ports before the armistice negotiations were completed. But the armistice, as signed, provided that France's Navy should fall under German control; and regretful, but resolute action had to be taken to prevent these ships being

used against Britain. On 3 July, two battleships, two light cruisers, many destroyers and nearly 200 smaller craft, including the world's largest submarine, the "Surcouf," were boarded and taken over, almost without resistance, by the British, who agreed that such of their crews as did not wish to continue the fight should be repatriated to France. Above are seen some of the French warships that were seized in British ports.

243

HISTORIC SCENE IN THE HOUSE OF COMMONS. Besides the ships taken over in British ports (pages 242-243), and those dealt with at Oran (page 246), Admiral Godfrey, the French naval commander at Alexandria, agreed to demilitarize the vessels there at the demand of the British; while at Dakar the battleship·

"Richelieu," which refused the British proposals, was sunk by the Fleet Air Arm on 8 July. In the picture above, specially drawn by Stephen Spurrier, Mr. Churchill, addressing Parliament on 4 July, has just described the measures so far taken, under sad necessity, to prevent the French fleet being used against Britain.

FRENCH SHIPS DESTROYED AT ORAN. At Oran lay two crack battleships, "Dunkerque" and "Strasbourg," with many other units of the French fleet. After unsuccessful parleys with Admiral Gensoul, the French officer in command, it became necessary for Vice-Admiral Sir James Somerville to open fire. Several French ships were sunk or damaged. The "Dunkerque" (above) was driven aground and later rendered useless by air bombardment. Below is a general view of the harbour at Oran where the action took place.

Hitler returns in triumph to Berlin

HITLER IN HIS CAPITAL. On 6 July Hitler returned to Berlin after eight weeks spent with the army in the field. Ordered by Reich Minister Goebbels to give the Fuehrer a welcome " such as Berlin had never seen before," to celebrate the successful conclusion of the German campaigns in France, large crowds were dragooned to cheer him on his progress through the city, accompanied by his usual squads of storm troopers and S.S. men. Above, Hitler can be seen standing up in the leading car to receive the "mechanized" welcome.

NEW CONSTITUTION FOR FRANCE. On 9 July the French Chamber of Deputies at Vichy voted for the reform of the Constitution by 395 votes to 3. Later the Senate confirmed this decision. So the way was paved for the overthrow of the Republic and for the welding of yet another dictatorship from the battered fragments of the Constitution. Above, the French National Assembly is seen in session when the democratic parliament voted itself out of existence. Below, M. Pierre Laval, Vice-Premier, on his way to the meeting.

Aircraft Minister appeals to Britain's women

APPEAL FOR ALUMINIUM. On 9 July Lord Beaverbrook, Minister of Aircraft Production, made an appeal to the women of Britain to give up their aluminium pots and pans to help the national effort to build fighter planes. "We want aluminium, and we want it now," said Lord Beaverbrook, for with the collapse of France a valuable source of aluminium had passed into enemy hands. The wonderful response can be judged from the lower picture. Above, is a part of one of the aircraft factories which reaped the benefit.

BRITISH NAVY ROUTS ITALIAN FLEET. The first major action between the British and Italian Fleets took place in the Mediterranean on 9 July. The enemy squadron, comprising two battleships and a number of cruisers and destroyers, put up a smoke screen as soon as the British appeared, and turned tail for home. Later the Italian news agency announced that their navy had fought a " glorious and successful action " with the British Navy. The pictures show (top) shells from the British squadron bursting near an Italian battleship, which is firing dead astern. Below, the guns of an Italian warship are seen firing during the engagement.

GERMAN TANKER SUNK. In spite of the loss of the French Channel ports, the British Navy and Air Force by combined operations retained the mastery of the whole of the English Channel and the Strait of Dover, through which convoy after convoy passed safely, bringing munitions and food supplies to British harbours. German shipping which attempted to sneak out of enemy-occupied ports continued to do so at its peril. In this picture, which is taken from an R.A.F. bomber, another plane of the squadron is shown flying above an enemy tanker bombed off the French coast and sinking in a mass of smoke and flames.

DEFENCE MEASURES IN THE UNITED STATES. Though preoccupied by the coming presidential elections, America showed itself during the months of June and July to be increasingly aware of the German threat to world democracy. Among many measures dictated for home defence was the calling up of volunteers for the army, who are seen at a training camp in the lower picture. Above, Colonel Knox is being sworn into his new appointment as Secretary of the United States Navy before President Roosevelt.

FRANCE'S DAY OF MOURNING. The 14th July, the anniversary of the Fall of the Bastille in 1789, is normally a day of national celebration in France. This year the crowds were sombre and dejected, as shown in the picture above of Bordeaux citizens standing in silence before the memorial to those killed in the last war. Below, General de Gaulle is reviewing a unit of his force after laying a wreath at the Cenotaph, where his words "Vive l'Angleterre, Vive la France," were taken up and re-echoed by the crowd.

AIR BATTLE OVER THE STRAIT OF DOVER.
One of the most determined attacks by the German
Air Force on British shipping in the Strait of Dover
was carried out on 14 July, when about forty dive
bombers escorted by fighters, took part. Although
at least seven enemy planes were destroyed, the
results of the raid were negligible for, as shown in
the picture, almost all the bombs fell into the sea.

(British Official Photograph: Crown Copyright Reserved)

Germans "we seek no terms and ask no mercy"

MR. CHURCHILL, IN HIS STIRRING
BROADCAST TO BRITAIN AND THE WORLD
ON 14 JULY, 1940 :—

"All goes to show that the war will be long and hard. No one can tell where it will spread. One thing is certain—the peoples of Europe will not be ruled for long by the Nazi Gestapo, nor will the world yield itself to Hitler's gospel of hatred and domination. . . .

"Here in this strong city of refuge, which enshrines the title deeds of human progress and is of deep consequence to Christian civilization; here, girt about by the seas and oceans where the Navy reigns, shielded from above by the staunchness and devotion of our airmen, we await undismayed the impending assault. . . .

"But be the ordeal sharp or long, or both, we shall seek no terms, we shall tolerate no parley. We may show mercy—we shall ask none."

BRITAIN PREPARES FOR INVASION. Undaunted by futile Nazi threats of annihilation, Britain prepared to defend herself against attack by sea or by air. Barbed wire entanglements were erected at strategic points, as shown on the left, where Big Ben is silhouetted behind its unaccustomed defence. Signposts were removed from all roads (above), and the streets of London (below) were barricaded and strongly guarded.

L.D.V.s PREPARE FOR THE REAL THING. The threat of invasion to Britain was responsible for the introduction of many stringent precautions. Amongst these was the erection of temporary barricades on all the main roads of Southern and Eastern England. These were put in position at night and manned by Local Defence Volunteers, who challenged and stopped all traffic for the examination of identification cards.

Such a barricade is seen in the picture on the top left. Bottom left, L.D.V.s are seen learning how to throw bottle bombs, or "Molotov Cocktails," which are used to deal with enemy tanks. Above, the effect of one of these " cocktails " on a dummy tank towed by a car is shown. The bombs, which are bottles partially filled with a mixture of petrol, paraffin and crude oil, were used with much success during the Finnish campaign.

BRITAIN ON GUARD. On 14 May, Mr. Eden had announced the formation of a Home Guard of Local Defence Volunteers. By the middle of July their number exceeded one million, many of them veterans of the last war determined to defend their country to the last ditch. Here an armed guard of L.D.V.s is patrolling an important point on Britain's system of railway communications, armed with rifle and bayonet, and wearing their official uniform, proving themselves to be Britain's "first reserves against invasion."

The activities of this new defence force were not restricted to the land. The Upper Thames Patrol, the "navy" of the Home Guard, kept watch by day and night on the locks, towpaths, bridges and landing steps of London's riverside. Its smart motor launches, most of which were privately owned and manned by amateur yachtsmen, patrolled altogether 125 miles of the Thames. Above, in a picturesque setting, is seen a flotilla of the patrol, its ships dressed, on its way to be reviewed by the Commander-in-Chief, Rear-Admiral Sir Basil Brooke.

" WE SHALL FIGHT ON THE BEACHES . . . WE SHALL NEVER SURRENDER." Following Mr. Churchill's words: "We shall defend our island whatever the cost may be. We shall fight on the beaches, we shall fight on the landing grounds, in the fields, in the streets and in the hills," Britain's people's moat was completed in record time and manned by a mixture of regular soldiers and L.D.V.s. The picture above shows a unit on tactical exercises on one of England's beaches in preparation for any attack which the enemy might hurl at us.

the island fortress

New weapons and defence methods were speedily forthcoming to deal with the threat of invasion. From June the entire output—5,000 per month, rapidly expanding—of the new American " gangster " weapon, the " Tommy " sub-machine gun, firing 1,500 rounds a minute from either shoulder or hip, was shipped weekly to Britain. Above, troops training with the new gun advance to attack. Below, a R.A.S.C. squad, brought up in lorries, searching among the heather for parachute troops during tactical exercises in Southern England.

"IRONSIDES" AWAIT THE ENEMY. Among the devices for dealing with the expected invader were the aptly-nicknamed "Ironsides," armoured cars of a new type, fitted with Bren guns. Some of the new cars, which can operate in the roughest country, are seen (above) moving off for exercises in an English park.

tanks keep in training

Britain made sure that, if Hitler was to be Britain's first invader for 900 years, he should find a mechanized army awaiting him, and that tanks, which he had exploited so successfully in France and the Low Countries, were as powerful a weapon in British hands. Above, light tanks taking a rise over open country in Southern England.

ACTIVITY ON THE WOMEN'S FRONT. As men in greater and greater numbers were absorbed into the defence forces, their womenfolk stepped forward not only to play a magnificent part in the drive in the munitions factories, to become bus conductors and postmen, to man the farms and bring in the harvest (above), but even formed an "Amazon Corps," later the Women's Volunteer Defence Corps, who learnt rifle drill (below) with sticks and umbrellas to take a share in defending themselves against the awaited invader.

King reviews New Zealanders

NEW ZEALAND TROOPS IN CAMP. On 6 July the King paid a visit to his New Zealand troops, including Maoris, under canvas in England. Below, he is seen inspecting gunners and infantrymen from the Dominion at drill and bayonet practice. At the conclusion of his visit he paid high compliment to their commanders, Major-Generals Johnson and Freyberg, on the fitness, smart appearance and excellent marching of their men. Above, a squad of the New Zealand Divisional Signals, undergoing training as motor cyclist dispatch riders.

Britain is told to

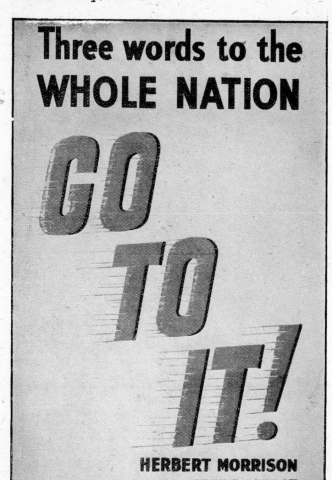

MR. HERBERT MORRISON, Minister of Supply, inaugurated a nation-wide campaign of increased efficiency with his speech broadcast on 22 May.

" Let us refresh ourselves with the realization of our own strength," he said.

" And let us express that strength now, tonight, tomorrow, every moment until victory is won. Work is the call. Work at war speed.

" What is needed, is an intense concentrated effort of muscle and mind and will, which must begin now.

" The job of my Ministry is to turn the wealth of the nation into bullets and shells and guns and tanks—to take the raw material of our great productive power and forge it into a sword of victory.

" Now that the full pressure of war is upon us, the drive behind the work must increase; its pace must quicken; its scope must extend. More shells, more tanks, more guns.

" You know what is at stake—you know what fate awaits us if those ruthless desperadoes succeed in making us the next victims of their juggernaut ride.

" The enemy's first blow against us at home is being struck now. As always, that first blow is his attempt to sow fear and confusion in our minds.

" We—all of us—will defeat that attempt.

" Goodnight—and go to it!"

"Go To It!"—and does

LABOUR'S GREAT SPEED-UP. Roused by the rallying calls of the Premier and of the new Labour Ministers, Mr. Bevin and Mr. Morrison, to put forth their utmost effort in defence of British freedom and British ways of life, men and women workers in every industry turned out munitions and arms in ever-growing quantity. Besides working overtime, they gave up their week-ends and, in many cases, their holidays, in a titanic effort to supply the needs of Britain's rapidly expanding fighting forces. Below (left), shipping workers, who are building five million tons of shipping to replace losses, leaving the yards. Above, women working presses in a sound locator factory. Below, vast furnaces turn scrap iron into high-grade steel.

MEN AND MACHINES AT THE DOUBLE. Spurred on by the call for unceasing output at whatever cost of toil, sweat and suspension of hard-won privileges, shift after shift of workers toiled amid the unceasing roar of machines in the hot summer days to double and redouble supplies for the men on the fighting front. Above, a Bren gun plant, with some of the 600 machines used in constructing these weapons. Below (right), adding the final touches in a tank factory. Above (right), one of the women workers in a munitions factory hard at work.

determines to deliver the goods

LABOUR MINISTER APPEALS TO THE WORKERS

In his first speech after his appointment as Minister of Labour, Mr. Ernest Bevin said:—

"I hope the War Cabinet will not allow vested interests, profits, or anything else to stand in the way of maximum production. If this is the policy of the Government, I will ask my people to work like hell to save the lives of our lads."

A few days later, addressing a meeting of workers and employers in the coal industry, he made a clarion call to British capital and labour.

"Do you want to shorten the war? Then give me your answer when you are at work by delivering the goods. Forget your own quarrels in the common effort. Every effort you make will be a valuable contribution to our success, so do not spare yourselves. . . .

"To the employers I say: You may in the past have been tempted to haggle about your fifteen per cent or your capital position. Remember, if Hitler wins, there will be no capital position. My appeal to you is: Don't worry about anything now but winning the war. I say the same to the men. We can very well sit down and talk about things afterwards. . . .

"We will deliver the goods. We will send the men and the material. Hold on, and victory is in sight."

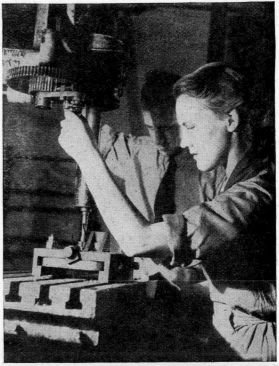

R.A.F. BOMB VITAL WATERWAY. The Dortmund-Ems Canal, an important artery in Germany's waterway system, was singled out as a special objective for the R.A.F., and a resolute attack was made on 18 July. Picked crews dropped bombs on the aqueduct carrying the canal over the River Ems. Above, the canal is seen before the raid; barges show white in the black streak (left to right) of the water-filled canal. Below, after the raid, bomb craters in the now empty canal and stranded barges at its sides show the effects of R.A.F. attentions.

(British Official Photographs: Crown Copyright Reserved)

R.A.F. WORRY GERMAN BASES. Night after night the bombers of the R.A.F. went forth on their work of destruction, wreaking havoc in German industrial centres and communication lines. Oil depots, aeroplane factories and aerodromes were their main objectives. Unlike the German Air Force, they concentrated entirely on military objectives and had orders to bring their bombs back rather than drop them at random on non-military areas. Above, a bombing crew is seen on its return from a night's work over Germany. Below, examining bombs in preparation for a night attack. *(British Official Photographs: Crown Copyright Reserved)*

SINKING OF "BARTOLOMEO COLLEONI." Australia's navy showed what it could do on 19 July, when H.M.A.S. "Sydney," with some destroyers, contacted the "Bartolomeo Colleoni" and another Italian cruiser off Crete. Sighted by the destroyers, "Colleoni" attempted escape, but "Sydney's" accurate fire scored vital hits which reduced her speed and allowed the British destroyers to finish her off. The second cruiser was chased and hit, but her speed enabled her to get away before she could be sent to join her sister

ship. Bombed meanwhile by Italian planes, the British ships rescued the crew from the doomed cruiser, including the captain; there were no British casualties. "Colleoni," a 5,000-ton cruiser of equivalent armament to "Sydney's," had a complement of 500 officers and men and was reported to have attained on trials a speed slightly in excess of 40 knots. Specially drawn by A. J. W. Burgess, R.I., the picture shows men taking off from the doomed ship to the safety of the British warships as Italian planes overhead impede the work of rescue.

" LANCASTRIA " SUNK BY GERMAN DIVE BOMBERS. On 25 July came the news of the sinking, by Junkers dive bombers of the Cunard-White Star liner "Lancastria"—well known to British holidaymakers as a cruising vessel—off St. Nazaire, while evacuating British troops from France on 17 June. About half of the

5,000 odd men on board, mostly British soldiers and airmen, were saved, in spite of the fact that the ship sank within half an hour of the attack. The picture above (left), taken from one of the ships that rushed to the rescue, shows men swimming for safety as she heels over preparatory to taking her death plunge.

French and Czech troops to fight for Britain

FOREIGN TROOPS RE-FORM IN ENGLAND. Throughout the summer the reconstruction on British soil of foreign units from the occupied countries proceeded apace. On 21 July, Britain recognized the Czechoslovak Government established in London. Above, Dr. Benes, its head, is saluting the colours at a review of Czech troops in Southern England. Below, men of the French Foreign Legion who, after fighting at Narvik escaped to England from Brittany, and joined General de Gaulle's Free French Army, march past at their English camp.

FAILURE OF AIR ATTACK ON DOVER.   The 29th July saw the biggest air fight so far off Britain's coast. Eighty German planes attempted a surprise raid on shipping in Dover Harbour; nineteen were destroyed by British fighters, and two by anti-aircraft batteries, against one British machine lost and two damaged. Not a single one of the raiders' bombs fell on land.   Above, bursting shells from anti-aircraft batteries are seen in the plane-studded sky as bombs explode in the water, well wide of the vessels at anchor.

TRANSFER OF AMERICAN DESTROYERS PROPOSED. On 4 August, General Pershing, Commander-in-Chief of American troops in Europe in 1917, lent his support in a broadcast to a campaign which had been organized in the U.S. advocating the sale to Britain of some fifty or sixty of the fleet of decommissioned destroyers, many of them reconditioned, which since the war of 1914-18, had been lying in harbour at

Philadelphia, where some of them are seen above. These ships would be of inestimable value to Britain as additional wartime flotillas. The suggestion was approved by the President though he felt unable to act on it until Republican support was forthcoming. Numbers of these ships were transferred to Britain early in September by a reciprocal arrangement in exchange for naval and air bases in British territories in the Atlantic.

POLAND'S NEW ARMY. On 5 August an agreement was signed providing for the reorganization of Poland's armed forces in Britain as a separate unit under the Allied High Command. Above, General Sikorski, Poland's Premier and Commander-in-Chief, decorates the banner of the Polish Highland Brigade, which fought at Narvik. Below, the British flying boat "Clare," which took off for America when Britain resumed the transatlantic air service on 4 August, unloading at an English port after her first double crossing to New York and back.

BRITISH TROOPS KEEP IN TRAINING. As Italian concentrations were massed for action on the Libyan border in early August, the British and Dominion troops in the Western Desert prepared to receive them, dealing destruction meanwhile on the Italian planes which raided Alexandria and the inland aerodromes and desert stations. Above, a British signal company training in the desert. Below, Egyptian gunners manning anti-aircraft guns at a coast defence post. *(British Official Photographs: Crown Copyright Reserved)*

SOMALILAND CAMEL CORPS ON PATROL. On 4 August, Italian forces invaded British Somaliland simultaneously from three points. British tactics in this inhospitable and difficult country were directed not to defending every inch of territory, but to harassing the invaders in all possible ways, compelling them to dissipate their forces. Doughty fighters for Britain were the Somaliland Camel Corps, now partly mechanized and armed with Bren guns, who put up a stubborn fight before Britain was forced to evacuate the country on 19 August. A patrol is here seen in the desert

PARIS AIRPORT RAIDED.　On 7 August, the pilot of a British bomber made a lone attack on the German-occupied aerodrome of Le Bourget, the airport of Paris.　Concealing himself behind clouds, he swooped down and dropped bombs on the tarmac, where several Nazi machines were standing.　Other bombs hit the hangars.　The defence was taken by surprise, and the British pilot made a "get-away" before the A.A. batteries had time to come into action.　The picture shows Nazi soldiers walking past some of the hangars.

Another reverse for Italian Navy

WAR IN THE MEDITERRANEAN. The British Navy and R.A.F. dealt repeated blows on the Italian fleet, which always showed itself readier to run than to fight, unless the British were greatly inferior in numbers. In one action in Maltese waters a squadron of British light cruisers tackled a detachment of the Duce's navy including battleships, cruisers and destroyers, damaging a battleship and a cruiser. Above, an Italian ship firing a broadside during the engagement. Below, havoc wrought in enemy battleship by a British shell.

AUSTRALIAN ARTILLERY AT WORK. Further drafts of the Australian Imperial Force arrived in Britain at the beginning of August, including medium and heavy artillery brigades. Above, some of these splendid fighters are training with a new tractor 25-pounder medium field gun, easily convertible into an anti-tank gun, with which some of their batteries are equipped. Below, another such gun is being loaded during a field display. Right, some Aussies have discovered that haystacks make very good [camouflage for their howitzers.

MEN FROM NEWFOUNDLAND MAN THE GUNS. Britain's oldest dominion was not prevented from playing her full part in the war by the economic crisis that for several years past had lain heavily upon her. Not only did many of her brave fishermen sail for England to join their British colleagues in the dangerous task of clearing home waters of German mines (see page 72) but several artillery units from Newfoundland came to take their place among the defending forces. Some of them are seen above manning a 9.2-inch howitzer.

BRITISH READY IN EGYPT. The threatened land attack on Egypt by the Duce's forces in Libya was slow to materialize, water supply difficulties in the Western Desert, over which the Italian troops must cross to reach their objective, dissuading their commanders from hurried action. Meanwhile the British forces defending the country perfected their arrangements for giving the invader, should he come, a hot reception. Above, a R.A.F. bomber formation on patrol over the Pyramids. Below, Egyptian troops in the desert haul a gun into position.

PREMIER VISITS TROOPS. In the intervals of organizing the nation's war effort from Downing Street, Mr. Churchill made several visits of inspection to defence works, coast fortifications and munition factories in various parts of the country, to congratulate troops and workers on their united effort and spur them on to even greater vigilance. Here he is inspecting a battalion of the Grenadier Guards with their Bren gun carriers, and (above) being saluted during a tour among the home defenders and munition workers of N.E. England.

AUSTRALIA PLEDGES ASSISTANCE TO THE END. The redoubled determination of every unit of the British Commonwealth to hold on until a final blow had been dealt to Nazi aspirations was emphasized anew as the German attack became wholly concentrated on Britain. Above, Australian ex-service men pledge allegiance to the national war effort before the Cenotaph in Sydney. Below, Australia's Parliament debates a National Emergency Bill by which the country's entire resources are placed at the Government's disposal.

ITALY'S AFRICAN PORTS BOMBARDED. Heavy attacks were made during July and August by the Navy and R.A.F. on Italian ports and supply bases on the Libyan coast, especially Derna, Tobruk and Bardia, the last Italy's main forward base for Western Desert operations. Above, an attacking cruiser off the Libyan shore. Below, a gun in action as units of the Mediterranean Fleet bombard a coast port. *(Movietone-Gaumont Newsreels)*

"WELLINGTON" BOMBER LOADS UP. The whole of Western Europe under German and Italian domination was every night the happy hunting ground of British bombing planes, whose operations extended from Norway to Italy, the vast width of the front open to them making it impossible for the enemy to anticipate their next stroke. Above, a train of 250-lb. bombs is being loaded into a "Wellington" in preparation for its night's work.

MASS RAIDS OVER BRITAIN. The air offensive against Britain started in full force on 8 August. From then until the 19th, when there was a temporary lull, bombers came over almost continuously, attacking aerodromes, dockyards, and munition works. High explosive and incendiary bombs were released over military and non-military objectives, but the damage done by the raiders, hopelessly outclassed by the British fighters and harried by a death-dealing barrage of anti-aircraft fire, was out of all proportion to the losses they suffered. The balloon barrage was singled out in the early raids as a special object of attack. Above, the trail of a barrage balloon shot down by enemy raiders off the S.E. coast. Right (below), another balloon in flames; its attacker can be seen on the right of the picture. Right (above), Nazi raiders scuttle for home as fighters intercept them.

blitzkrieg begins

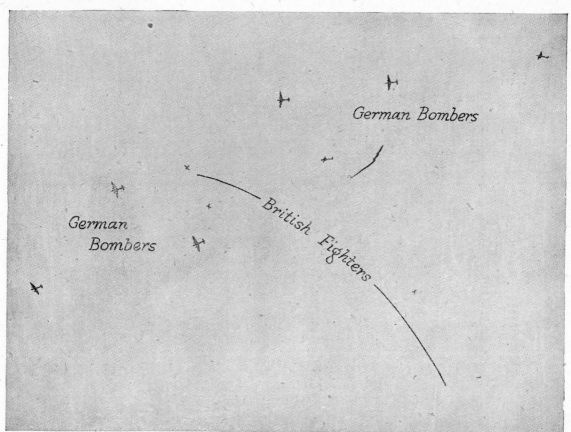

HEAVY COST OF AIR BLITZKRIEG.
The phenomenal successes of the British fighter pilots in their combats with the Nazi raiders were due in large measure to their unbounded faith in their machines. Both the "Hurricane" and the "Spitfire" fighters proved themselves time and time again to be faster and more manœuvrable than their German counterparts, besides possessing a more powerful and more devastating armament in their eight machine guns. In spite of their best efforts the Messerschmitts escorting the German bombers failed to keep their more nimble opponents at bay or to prevent them from taking a terrible toll of their bomber formations. Above, a Dornier "flying pencil" bomber, its engine aflame, diving to destruction after an encounter with a British fighter. Below, a Nazi airman, whose parachute failed to open when he "baled out" after the tail of his machine was shot off, crashes on a housetop.

Dornier shot down by Home Guard

HOME GUARD'S FIRST VICTIM. Not all the spoils of the war over Britain fell to the regulars. On 18 August a detachment of the Home Guard, from their sandbagged emplacement on the South London outskirts, claimed the first bomber, a Dornier, to fall to the volunteer defenders. They shot it down after 180 rounds of rifle fire. Above are some of the men who shot the bomber down. Below is the result of their lunch-hour labours.

WRECKAGE OF THE LUFTWAFFE. The accumulation of scrap material from planes shot down in Britain became almost embarrassing to the authorities, and a central dump (above) was established where the useful

Planes lost in fighting over Britain and the coast, 8–19 August, 1940 (R.A.F. official figures)

	German planes lost	British planes lost	British pilots safe
August 8	61	18	3
„ 9	1	—	—
„ 10	1	1	—
„ 11	65	26	2
„ 12	62	13	1
„ 13	78	13	10
„ 14	31	7	2
„ 15	180	34	17
„ 16	75	22	14
„ 17	1	—	—
„ 18	152	22	8
„ 19	4	—	—
TOTAL	**711**	**156**	**57**

material was sorted out for conversion in due course into new British planes. On the right, workmen are seen enjoying their midday meal in the wrecked fuselage of a bomber collected from Goering's air armada.

GERMAN SHELLS FAIL TO DAMAGE BRITISH SHIPPING. In early August, German high-velocity guns were massed along the French coast from Calais to Boulogne, which would serve to cover troop transports in an attempt at invading Britain. On the 22nd these guns were brought into action for the first time against a convoy in the Channel, firing a shell a minute for over an hour as the ships passed through the narrows—and

missing every time. Nazi dive bombers, simultaneously attacking the convoy and its escort from above, were equally unsuccessful, for the skilful seamanship of the British vessels, combined with the accurate fire of the escorting warships, made close approach too hazardous. As the salvos from the German coastal batteries fell harmlessly around the ships (above), British destroyers laid smoke screens and dropped smoke floats (below).

GUNS SHELL DOVER FROM FRENCH COAST. The cross-channel guns followed up their attack on Channel shipping by bombarding the coast in the neighbourhood of Dover for about three-quarters of an hour on the evening of the 22nd, damaging some buildings, including a church whose interior is shown above and inflicting several casualties. The R.A.F. immediately replied by raiding the gun emplacements, dropping

high explosive and incendiary bombs on the neighbourhood of Cape Gris Nez amid heavy enemy anti-aircraft fire. British heavy guns from the Kent coast also responded to the fire across Channel. Above, members of Dover's civil defence services are seen examining a shell crater in a road, close to another church. The force of the explosion can be judged by the damage caused to the front of the house on the right of the picture.

NAZI BOMBS DON'T WORRY LONDON. If the purpose of the mass raiding was to undermine the Londoner's morale, it was a ludicrous failure. Munition factories carried on work as bombs fell near them, and in many cases repair work on damaged buildings began within an hour or two of the passing of the Nazi planes. In public shelters men and women played cards or sang, while many thousands, turning over in bed with a word of annoyance as the sirens sounded for another "all-night" raid, settled to sleep again, undisturbed by anti-aircraft fire, until the "raiders passed" signal woke them once more. Above, nuns arrive at a scarred railway station in a bombed suburb to help in rescue work after a raid. Below, the interior of a suburban cinema after it had received a direct hit from a Nazi bomb.

END OF A MESSERSCHMITT. The R.A.F. and the anti-aircraft defences rejoiced in the opportunity given by the August raids to decimate Goering's "invincible" Luftwaffe, and in ten days accounted for 711 Nazi planes (see table on page 301), not bothering to count the probably even greater number so badly mauled that it was unlikely that they could have returned to their bases. The picture above shows one of many German fighters brought down by "Hurricanes" and "Spitfires" burning itself out in open parkland in S.E. England.

AIR WAR REACHES THE CITY. On 16 August, London was first bombed by Nazi raiders who hit several buildings in the S.W. suburbs including churches, a hospital and a railway station, and opened machine gun fire on people in the streets. The Nazi wireless admitted that orders had been given to the attacking force to bomb the City "if necessary." Croydon Airport was a special objective of the attacks, and on 15 August it was assaulted by about thirty dive bombers, who secured a hit on a hangar and destroyed a number of houses

in the immediate neighbourhood. Swift retribution followed, for not a single plane that took part in the Croydon bombing returned to Germany. London's anti-aircraft guns first came into action on 18 August, when delayed action bombs were dropped in the suburbs. It was not until the 25th, however, after many reconnaissance flights, that enemy machines succeeded in penetrating the outer defences and reaching the inner districts where they bombed a City building, the flames from which illuminate the night sky behind the dome of St. Paul's.

FIREMEN TACKLE CITY BLAZE. On 25 August, just after midnight, the first bombs were dropped on the City, causing a fire which gutted a large commercial building. Left, firemen are playing on the blaze from a water tower. Above, the fire under control. Several hundred bombs were dropped on and near London during five raids in the space of thirty hours, but the damage that resulted was small and of no military importance.

RAIDERS OVER S.E. ENGLAND. On 26 August, three waves of enemy bombers and fighters carried out raids on South-East England, especially over Portsmouth, the Thames Estuary and Folkestone. In the latter town a formation of about twenty planes dive bombed to about 500 feet, machine gunning streets, demolishing several houses on the sea front, and securing two direct hits on a laundry where three persons were killed. The raiders

were immediately attacked by British fighter pilots, assisted by Canadian squadrons and also by the newly formed Czech air force. Four enemy machines were shot down and altogether the day's bag amounted to at least forty-six enemy machines brought down against a loss of fifteen British fighters, eleven of whose pilots were saved by their parachutes. The above picture shows bombs bursting during the attack on Folkestone.

ALL-NIGHT RAID ON BRITAIN'S CAPITAL. Goering's air force launched its first all-night raid on London, when on the night of 26 August small waves of Nazi bombers operated repeatedly over the London area from 9.30 p.m. to 3.45 a.m. Though bombs were dropped in residential districts over a wide area, the resulting damage was small and out of all proportion to the "nuisance value" of the attack, and the main purpose of the raid seemed to be to hold up production by depriving workers of their sleep—though it took more than anti-aircraft fire and the fall of incendiary bombs to keep many stolid Londoners out of bed! The most illustrious victim claimed by the Nazis on this occasion was John Milton, whose statue outside the City church where he is buried was blown from its pedestal by bomb blast and slightly damaged. A.R.P. workers are seen (left, below) tending the poet's wounds. Left (above), the wreckage of a Heinkel bomber which fell in flames in the garden of a bungalow on London's outskirts without, however, injuring the occupants. Searchlights sweeping the heavens in chase of the marauders (above) gave Londoners a wonderfully vivid display of sky patterns.

MORE AND MORE MEN FROM THE EMPIRE. As the first year of the war drew to a close more and more of the Empire's man-power was mobilized to swell the ranks of those who were engaged in the struggle for freedom. Many troops from British territories overseas were already in the Mother Country awaiting the long-expected invader, whilst others in remote corners of the earth were mustering their strength to join battle

when the call came. Early in August the first detachments of the South African Field Force arrived in East Africa. Below (left) South African soldiers parading to hear an address by General Smuts, the Union Premier, on the eve of embarkation for the north; (right), a loaded transport about to depart from a Union port. Above, Indian troops from the State of Patiala reviewed before leaving India for active service overseas.

EUROPE
AFTER ONE YEAR OF WAR

AXIS POWERS SEPT. 1 1939 _ _ _ _ _ _ _ _

AXIS POWERS OCCUPIED TERRITORY SEPT. 1 1940

RUSSIAN OCCUPIED TERRITORY SEPT. 1 1940 _ _ _ _

BULGARIAN OCCUPIED TERRITORY SEPT. 1 1940 _ _ _ _

BOUNDARIES SEPT. 1 1939 _____   BOUNDARIES SEPT. 1 1940 _ _ _ _ _ _

SCALE OF MILES

0   100   200   300   400   500   600   700

NORTHERN IRELAND

EIRE

BRITISH ISLES

LONDON

CHANNEL IS.

ATLANTIC

OCEAN

NORTH

DENMARK

SEA

SWEDEN

NORWAY

BALTIC S

DANZIG

PR

BERLIN

WARSA

GERMANY

PO

HOLLAND

BELGIUM

LUXEMBURG

PARIS

FRANCE

VICHY

SWITZ?

BOHEMIA

MORAVIA

SLOVAK

AUSTRIA

HUNGA

PORTUGAL

MADRID

SPAIN

CORSICA

ROME

SARDINIA

ITALY

YUGO

SLAVI

ALBANIA

GIBRALTAR

SPAN. MOROCCO

MEDITERRANEAN

SICILY

SEA

MOROCCO

ALGERIA

TUNIS

MALTA

WAR CHANGES THE FACE OF TWO CONTINENTS. When war broke out in September, 1939, Germany already had been responsible for several changes in the map of Europe. Austria, Czechoslovakia and Memel had been incorporated within the Third Reich. After the outbreak of war Poland was overrun and shared between Germany and Russia, and the latter widened her frontier still further after the war with Finland. Then, in April, Germany occupied Norway and Denmark and in the following two months overran most of France and the Low Countries in a lightning campaign. In June, Russia demanded Bessarabia and Bukovina from Rumania and occupied these areas on the 28th. Russia won a political rather than geographical victory in July, when the

S·J·Turner, F.R.G.S.

Baltic States Estonia, Latvia and Lithuania, over which she had been steadily increasing her influence, decided to become Soviet republics. In August, Rumania was forced to cede more territory; she handed over Southern Dobruja to Bulgaria and agreed to cede about sixty per cent of Transylvania to Hungary. Hungary, however, had not occupied this area by the end of the first year of the war. Meanwhile, in Africa, the Italians were in control of French Somaliland and had occupied British Somaliland, but political changes in favour of Britain took place towards the end of August, when the whole of French Equatorial Africa and the mandated territory of the Cameroons decided to throw in their lot with General de Gaulle, leader of the Free French Forces in Britain.

We shall never Surrender

EVEN though large tracts of Europe and many old and famous states have fallen or may fall into the grip of the Gestapo, and all the odious apparatus of Nazi rule, we shall not flag or fail. We shall go on to the end; we shall fight . . . on the seas and oceans; we shall fight with growing confidence and growing strength in the air; we shall defend our island whatever the cost may be. We shall fight on the beaches; we shall fight on the landing grounds; we shall fight in the fields and in the streets; we shall fight in the hills. We shall never surrender.

Extract from Prime Minister's Speech of June 4, 1940.